WALKING IN CORSICA
LONG-DISTANCE AND SHORT WALKS

ABOUT THE AUTHOR

Gillian Price was born in England but moved to Australia when young. After taking a degree in anthropology and working in adult education, she set off to travel through Asia and trek the Himalayas. The culmination of her journey was Venice, where her enthusiasm for mountains made the next logical step the Dolomites, only hours away. Starting there, Gillian has steadily explored the mountain ranges of Italy, and now Corsica, and brought them to life for visitors in a series of outstanding guides for Cicerone.

When not out exploring and photographing with her Venetian cartographer husband, Gillian works as a writer and translator. An adamant promoter of the use of public transport to minimise impact in alpine areas, she is also an active member of the Italian Alpine Club and the Outdoor Writers' Guild.

Other Cicerone guidebooks by Gillian Price
Walking in the Central Italian Alps
Walking in the Dolomites
Shorter Walks in the Dolomites
Treks in the Dolomites
Walking in Sicily
Walking in Tuscany
Trekking in the Apennines – The Grande Escursione Appenninica
Through the Italian Alps – The Grande Traversata delle Alpi
Across the Eastern Alps: E5
Gran Paradiso: Alta Via 2 Trek and Day Walks
Italy's Sibillini National Park: Walking and Trekking Guide
Walks and Treks in the Maritime Alps

WALKING IN CORSICA
LONG-DISTANCE AND SHORT WALKS

by
Gillian Price

CICERONE

2 POLICE SQUARE, MILNTHORPE, CUMBRIA LA7 7PY
www.cicerone.co.uk

© Gillian Price 2003
Reprinted with amendments 2006, 2010 (with updates)
ISBN 1 85284 387 8
ISBN-13: 978 1 85284 387 8

Maps: Nicola Regine
Photos: Gillian Price

Printed by KHL Printing, Singapore

A catalogue record for this book is available from the British Library.

Dedication

For Betty 'la courageuse' and Dave, inimitable chauffeur
(when he remembered to wear his glasses)

Acknowledgements

Many thanks to Walt Unsworth, who first suggested I went to 'la belle île',
to Giovanna for getting me there, and to Nicola, who has worked his
magic on the maps, yet again.

Advice to Readers

Readers are advised that, while every effort is made by our authors to ensure the accuracy of guidebooks as they go to print, changes can occur during the lifetime of an edition. Please check Updates on this book's page on the Cicerone website (www.cicerone.co.uk) before planning your trip. We would also advise that you check information about such things as transport, accommodation and shops locally. Even rights of way can be altered over time. We are always grateful for information about any discrepancies between a guidebook and the facts on the ground, sent by email to info@cicerone.co.uk or by post to Cicerone, 2 Police Square, Milnthorpe LA7 7PY, United Kingdom.

Front cover: Amazing views from Capu Rossu (Walk 6)

CONTENTS

Sketch Map Legend

════════ sealed road	crest
─ ─ ─ ─ ─ walk route	major watercourse
▬▬▬▬▬ walk route via sealed road	gîte d'étape/hotel
.... walk variant	tower
┼──□──┼ railway & station	church or shrine
	unmanned refuge

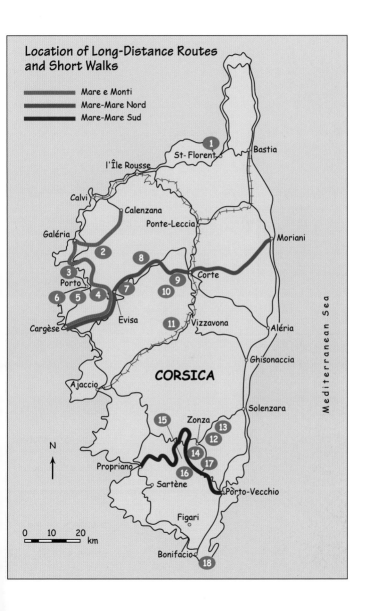

Location of Long-Distance Routes and Short Walks

- Mare e Monti
- Mare-Mare Nord
- Mare-Mare Sud

St-Florent — ①
Bastia

l'Île Rousse

Calvi

Calenzana

Ponte-Leccia

Galéria — ②

Moriani

③ Porto

⑧

⑥ ⑤ ④ ⑦

⑨ Corte

⑩

Cargèse

Evisa

⑪ Vizzavona

Aléria

Ghisonaccia

CORSICA

Ajaccio

Solenzara

N

⑮ Zonza
⑬
⑫
⑭
⑰

Propriano

⑯

Sartène

Pòrto-Vecchio

Figari

0 10 20 km

Bonifacio

⑱

Mediterranean Sea

Precarious Bonifacio on the ragged coastline (Walk 18)

INTRODUCTION

'The land of the vendetta, the siesta, complicated political games, potent cheeses, wild pigs, chestnuts, succulent blackbirds and ageless old men who watch life go by'

R. Goscinny and A. Uderzo,
Asterix in Corsica

Add to the above rugged mountain ranges, crystal-clear rivers, turquoise coves, romantic forests, the unforgettable scents of the maquis scrub, easygoing people, comfortable hostels and refuges, together with a host of well-marked paths, and you have, in a nutshell, an unparalleled paradise for walkers.

Its shores lapped by the Tyrrhenian and Ligurian seas, Corsica is the fourth largest island in the Mediterranean after Sicily, Sardinia and Cyprus. It has a surface area of 8682km² (3352 square miles), is 183km (113.7 miles) long and 83km (51.5 miles) wide, and is blessed with a stunning 1000km (621.3 mile) coastline. Moreover, some two-thirds of the land mass is taken up by an ancient mountain chain punctuated by a good 20 peaks well over 2000m (6500ft), while one-fifth is forested, and since 1972 a sizeable regional nature park has covered a vast 3500km² (1351 square mile) central swath of the island.

Corsica – or Corse in French – is administered by France, despite the fact that it is closer to Italy in both cultural and physical terms. A mere 90km (56 miles) separate it from the Tuscan coast, not to mention the narrow 11km (7 mile) strait with Sardinia, while it lies 170km (105 miles) from the Côte d'Azur in the south of France. The population of approximately 260,000 includes large numbers of mainlanders, along with a sizeable percentage of people of North African and Italian origin, drawn by work. In contrast it is said that due to unemployment more native Corsicans live in France than on the island itself.

Fanciful tales abound to explain the island's name. Phoenicians, the first seafarers to arrive, apparently referred to it as Ker-Cic ('slender promontory'). The Greeks came a little later and for them it was Kurnos ('covered with forests'). Legendary Greco-Roman hero Heracles put in there after labouring to fetch the golden apples at the world's end. He left one of his offspring, Kyrnos, in charge – hence the name. Perhaps the most colourful story comes courtesy of Roman mythology, wherein it belonged to a maiden called Corsa who had swum across from Liguria in pursuit of a runaway bull! Continuing the worldwide need for an explanation for events and naturally occurring phenomena, to this day island

View to Girolata and Capo Senino from Punta Literniccia (Mare e Monti)

life is infused with incredible accounts of miracle-working native saints at odds with ghostly spirits and the gruesome acts of the devil.

Corsica's very first inhabitants are believed to have migrated from north Italy around 7000BC. These hunters and gatherers developed into herders, and were joined by later arrivals responsible for the prehistoric menhirs and dolmens dotted through the hills. As is the fate of settled islands, vulnerable by their very nature, Corsica was raided periodically by Saracens and Barbary pirates, then occupied at length by the Pisans, who left some lovely Romanesque churches, and the Genoese, who stayed from the 13th century through to 1768, when they ceded it to France at a price, leaving a heritage of memorable citadels, watchtowers and bridges. In the meantime island-wide rebellions had

produced an enlightened period of autonomy under Pasquale Paoli (1755–69), concluding curiously at the same time as the birth of Napoleon Bonaparte at Ajaccio. There were also limited stretches under English sovereignty, as well as occupation by the forces of Italy and Germany during the Second World War when soldiers all but outnumbered locals. The ongoing independence movement, fiery at times, has dropped off considerably of late. It won 24% of votes in 1992 but a mere 16% in 1999. A 1990 French statute gave the island limited autonomy, however a greater measure was narrowly rejected in a historic 2003 referendum. There continues to be occasional violence from Corsican separatists.

Corsica is catching up with the rest of France and Europe in leaps and bounds in terms of standard of living, though figures remain marginally lower in terms of income, schooling and employment. The lack of industrial development, a negative factor in the past, is now turning into an advantage as visitors are attracted to this unspoilt paradise. Tourism is rapidly becoming a major factor in the economy, alongside livestock and agriculture, with cork, tobacco, wine, citrus fruit and olive oil all being produced for export.

WHEN TO GO

Any time of year is suitable to walk the coastal routes, thanks to the typical Mediterranean climate (although in winter there are fewer hotels and hostels open). In midsummer, however, you'd need to start out very early and take a break during the heat of the day. July and August can be unbearably hot in lowland areas, although proximity to the coast is unfailingly accompanied by a cooling

sea breeze. The spring period from March/April through to May can be simply divine, and will more than satisfy wild flower enthusiasts. This flowering period extends well into June for the mountainous interior. Once the winter snow has melted and paths are freed, the higher altitudes are at their photogenic best and provide a deliciously cool contrast to the heat elsewhere. July boasts the highest monthly average in terms of sunshine, with 11.9 hours per day! However, combined with August it also sees 70% of the tourist influx, so accommodation in popular spots must be pre-booked. On the other hand, these peak months do offer the advantage of more frequent public transport. One aspect of midsummer requires a warning note – walkers need to be aware of the unfortunately frequent danger of forest and scrub fires (see 'Dos and Don'ts' below).

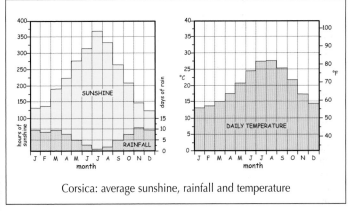

Corsica: average sunshine, rainfall and temperature

Corte's citadel (Mare-Mare Nord)

For the **weather forecast** (*météo* in French) call ☎08 92680220 or log onto www.meteo.fr and click on Corsica.

This ancient Corsican proverb may come in handy:

Arcu da sera, tempu si spera.

Arcu da mane, acqua à funtane which translates roughly as 'Rainbow in the evening, hope for good weather. Rainbow in the morning, fountains of water' (rain!).

GETTING TO CORSICA

Air

Most flights to Corsica entail a stopover in France before flying into either Bastia or Ajaccio. Some charter companies also fly into Figari near Bonifacio in the south, or Calvi on the west coast (perfect for the start of the Mare e Monti trail).

Sea

Ferries ranging from gigantic container-like vessels through to sleek, fast catamarans link the French mainland ports of Marseille and Nice all year round with Bastia and Ajaccio. These are supplemented by summer services to resort towns l'Île Rousse and Propriano on the west coast, along with Porto-Vecchio in the east. The majority carry vehicles as well as passengers. From Italy the main ports of departure are Genoa and Livorno, with ferries bound for Bastia and Porto-Vecchio. The main shipping lines are Corsica Ferries (www.corsica ferries.com), the Société Nationale Corse–Méditerranée (www.sncm.fr) and Moby Lines (www.mobylines.it). Advance booking for vehicles is essential in summer.

LOCAL TRANSPORT

Corsica is fairly easy to get around by public transport if you're not in a great hurry and don't mind the odd delay. A long list of private companies run mini-buses and long-distance coaches (referred to as *autocars* or simply *cars*) all over the island. Tourist offices in key tourist centres such as Bastia and Ajaccio distribute exhaustive sheets summarising all the lines relevant to their region. In minor towns the companies are usually based at travel agencies, where destinations and departure times will hopefully be on display. Otherwise try the local café – people are invariably helpful. Fares tend to be pretty steep and tickets are generally sold on board. Punctuality is another story, so don't plan a tight schedule if you have a plane or ferry to catch. The helpful website www.corsicabus.org has many bus routes and timetables.

Hitch-hiking is a piece of cake; depending on traffic flow, you rarely have to wait long for a lift from benevolent tourists or locals, particularly if you look like a hiker and are carrying a rucksack. However, as is the rule the world over, it is inadvisable for women to hitchhike on their own.

Most villages have a taxi service, but drivers seem to require lengthy advance warning and do not come cheap.

Train

The Chemins de Fer de la Corse, alias U Trinighellu or the *micheline*, is a marvellous narrow-gauge railway line that runs through the mountainous centre of Corsica connecting Bastia and Ajaccio with a branch line to Calvi on the west coast. It originally extended down the eastern seaboard to Porto-Vecchio, but the track was damaged by bombing in the Second World War and unfortunately never rebuilt. The train is handy for walkers heading for Calvi and the Mare e Monti trail, and is the perfect leisurely means of transport to reach Corte, strategically located for many mountain routes. A must for train buffs and others alike, it makes for a memorable rattling trip and is irreverently referred to as the island's TGV – Train Grande Vibration! Pocket timetables are widely available, otherwise call ☎04 95328060 for information. Remember that this

The following **glossary** will help in deciphering timetables:

quotidien, *tous les jours*	daily
sauf	except
seulement	only
jours fériés	Sunday and public holidays
lundi	Monday
mardi	Tuesday
mercredi	Wednesday
jeudi	Thursday
vendredi	Friday
samedi	Saturday
dimanche	Sunday

service is not renowned for its punctuality either.

The most thrilling stretch of track negotiates the narrow valley between the stations of Corte and Vizzavona, with a spectacular succession of viaducts, switchbacks and tunnels, looping back on itself for the climb to the 1000m mark. Renowned French civil engineer Gustave Eiffel was responsible for the 1888 design of the noteworthy steel girder bridge in the proximity of Vivario station.

Car

Car rental agencies are plentiful in the main towns and ports, though of course you can bring your own car on the spacious ferries (with the appropriate paperwork and insurance). The French road identification system uses the letter N for the more important *nationale* routes and D for relatively minor *départementale* roads, plus a distinguishing number. There are few straight routes on the island, so getting from A to B will take longer than you'd think. Visitors will find they spend a lot of time on twisting narrow roads, not often equipped with a guard rail and frankly hair-raising at times. Don't hesitate to sound your horn at blind corners in the interests of safety. The locals tend to ignore bends in the road so their vehicles often need dodging too. A further potential hazard for drivers is posed by wandering livestock, who deposit skid traps on the tarmac for unwary motorists.

This guide is intended to give a taste of the paradise Corsica offers walkers with its wonderful network of pathways. Three time-tested long-distance routes are described in detail, as is a selection of shorter walks designed as day-trips. However, it will quickly become clear to enterprising visitors that anyone suitably equipped and armed with a good measure of common sense, together with the appropriate detailed map, can 'do their own thing' and explore the multitudinous well-marked paths independently.

Walking in Corsica covers a vast range of the terrain – rough stony mountainsides and exposed airy ridges, slippery rock slabs, easy earth-based paths in wood and grassy pasture, sandy beaches and multitudinous river crossings – fords more often than not. A bit of everything!

How to Use this Guide

Most paths have clear waymarking, though numbering is rare. This is generally a regular succession of painted stripes on trees or prominent rocks, occasionally accompanied by an arrow and name of a landmark ahead. During the walk descriptions in this guide, 'track' is used to refer to an unsealed vehicle-width lane, while a 'path' is narrow and for pedestrians only. A 'road' is sealed, and traffic can be expected.

The individual route descriptions include the altitude (metres above sea

At Bocca Rezza (Mare e Monti)

level) of useful landmarks along the way (altitude is abbreviated as 'm' and given in brackets; minutes is abbreviated as 'min'). Compass directions as well as directional instructions 'right' and 'left' are supplied as an extra aid.

The timing given at the start of each walk does not include rest breaks or time out for taking photographs, so always add extra when planning your day's load. On level ground an averagely fit person will cover 5km (about 3 miles) in 1 hour. Timing given during the walk description is partial (ie. from the last reference point), unless otherwise specified. Some walkers may wish to combine some of the day stages in the long-distance walks in line with their fitness and availability of accommodation.

An entry for height gain and loss (ascent/descent) can be found in each walk heading (except where the ground is mostly flat) and is an

important indicator of the type of itinerary. Combined with the distance covered, it furnishes an idea of the effort required. Generally speaking, 300m (about 1000ft) in ascent is feasible in 1 hour. For the long-distance routes, these details can be found under the individual day headings along with the distance. Moreover, for anyone who finds it more convenient to follow them in the reverse direction, estimated times have been included in the 'Route Summaries' at the end of the guide, together with information about transport, accommodation and shops.

Place names will be encountered in varieties of French–Corsican–Italian, and disparities are regularly encountered between maps and actual signposts. Small villages and hamlets are important landmarks especially on the long-distance trails, however few have identifying signposts and there isn't often anyone to ask. One unfailingly reliable system for finding out where you are is to locate the cenotaph, as each village sent its sons to the conflicts France was engaged in, and the village name appears there.

Several stretches of the long-distance walks described in this guide have been adapted as day-walks with a return to base, and are described separately. However visitors with two cars at their disposal can follow virtually any stretch of the long-distance routes with a little advance planning. More ambitious, experienced walkers may want to undertake the renowned long-distance route the Grande Randonnée GR20, which traverses the island from Calenzana in the northwest to Conca in the southeast in 15 stages. It entails countless scrambles as the route climbs amidst top mountain scenery, but the 'downside' is that walkers need to be experienced as well as largely self-sufficient in terms of water, food and sleeping gear. Paddy Dillon's detailed guide *GR20 Corsica – The High-Level Route* is available from Cicerone.

In addition to the selection of walks described in this guide, interesting suggestions can be found in the brochures 'Balades en Corse – Sentiers du Pays', put out by the Parc Naturel Régional de Corse and available at local tourist offices. However they give no route details and a map is essential. Many routes are signposted at the very start then you are quickly left to your own devices.

Difficulty

A scale of 1 to 3 has been used to grade the walks in terms of difficulty.

- **Grade 1** indicates fairly easy going on mostly level ground, a broad track or clear path. Unless otherwise specified, it is suitable for all age groups and abilities.

- **Grade 2** is average, involving a fair amount of height gain and loss: basic orienteering skills may be required.

- **Grade 3** is challenging and is intended for seasoned walkers with stamina. Some experience on rocky terrain and exposure is recommended, along with orientation and map-reading skills.

Dos and Don'ts

Walking boots should be neither too new (blisters!) or too old (insufficient grip on stony terrain).

Don't overload your rucksack, as a sore back can spoil your holiday. An excessive load can also put you off balance on exposed ridges or during steep descents. Be honest - are you really going to have the time or energy to read that novel? Are those extra clothes really essential? (Corsica is a relaxed holiday destination and the need for 'dressing up' is rare.) It's enlightening to weigh your pack before setting out on long-distance routes – if it exceeds 10kg, think again.

Take both weather forecasts and fire warnings seriously and be prepared to modify your walk route if needs be. In the unfortunate event that you experience one of the island's infamous violent summer storms, complete with unbelievably torrential rain and potentially dangerous lightning, keep well away from prominent trees, rock overhangs, caves and metal fixtures (get rid of your trekking poles), and curl up on the ground keeping your head down. If on the other hand you are caught out by fire, take cover if possible in a watercourse, or on a high point where rescuers can spot you easily. If you notice a fire burning alert the authorities by phoning ☎ 18 (the *pompiers*, fire brigade) or ☎ 112 (general emergency number). Remember that lighting a fire out in the open is strictly forbidden from July through to September, though a total fire ban may be in force for a longer period.

Take care when fording rivers after heavy rain. Even the most sluggish watercourse can swell in a surprisingly short time and produce an impetuous flow. A stick or trekking pole will aid balance.

When crossing suspension bridges, one person at a time is the best rule, and the same goes for aided rock passages with fixed chain.

Don't plan your walk in too rigid a manner, as it will limit your flexibility. Allow for rest days and breaks for detours to places of interest instead of rushing straight through.

Carry plenty of drinking water at all times of year. When settlements are touched on, you'll nearly always get a refill, as true to farming tradition it's a very rare village that has no public drinking fountain or tap. Natural watercourses abound; however, so does grazing livestock, so drinking from streams is not always advisable.

Never proceed too far without checking for waymarking, as lack thereof may mean a wrong turn onto one of the many hunter's or boar trails. The long-distance routes are especially well marked with orange paint stripes.

Be considerate when making a toilet stop. Keep away from watercourses and never leave unsightly paper or tissues lying around. Derelict buildings or rock overhangs are also out – remember that they could serve as emergency shelter for someone!

Residents in the EU should take with them the European Health Insurance Card (EHIC), which replaces the E111 and entitles the holder to reciprocal health treatment in France. A 'Health Advice for Travellers' leaflet is available at post offices in the UK. Travel insurance covering a walking holiday is also recommended, and is essential for non-Europeans.

Last but not at all least behave as a responsible walker and leave nothing behind you except footprints.

Walking boots take a bashing in Corsica

In case of danger
Call the general emergency number
☎ 112. The French for 'help!' is 'au secours!'

WHAT TO TAKE

- sturdy walking boots with ankle support and non-slip soles
- a comfortable rucksack and a supply of plastic bags to keep everything dry
- T-shirts and shorts
- pullover and windproof jacket
- long trousers to protect your legs from the scratchy maquis shrubs
- waterproofs - either a voluminous poncho or separate jacket, over-trousers and rucksack cover. A lightweight fold-up umbrella will be appreciated by walkers who wear glasses

- sandals or flip-flops for beaches, dormitory wear and fording rivers
- sleeping sheet and towel
- sun-block cream, lip salve and a wide-brimmed hat
- trekking poles, preferably telescopic, handy for discouraging the odd over-enthusiastic dog, balancing on stepping stones during river crossings and hanging out your washing, not to mention diverting your rucksack load onto your arms
- first-aid kit, including antiseptic cream to treat grazes from brambles and maquis, and the odd nettle sting
- salt tablets to combat excessive sweating and fatigue
- a compass and even an altimeter,

Cucuruzzu affords lovely views over the Alta Rocca area (Walk 15)

combined with the appropriate walking map, are a great help should you inadvertently stray off the track
• swimming costume and goggles or mask

MAPS

A detailed contour map is an essential aid to any walk undertaken in Corsica. The sketch maps provided in this guide are limited by space and graphics and are not intended as substitutes. Excellent maps published by the France's Institute Géographique National (IGN) are referred to in the heading of each walk described in this book. The blue Top 25 1:25,000 series are on sale all over Corsica in newsagents and even supermarkets, not to mention outdoor and map shops overseas. An orange 1:50,000 series has also been published, handy for the long-distance routes, however they are inexplicably unavailable on the island and can only be purchased at official IGN outlets in France, through specialist distributors in other countries or online at www.ign.fr. At a stretch the green IGN 1:100,000 series could accompany a long-distance route and be used for identifying distant ranges and landmarks including villages, though they won't be much help if you get lost.

ACCOMMODATION

The wonderful French invention the *gîte d'étape*, walkers' hostel, is widespread in Corsica. Unfailingly

Price list at a gîte d'étape

great places to meet people, they provide a shower and multi-course evening meal at the end of a day's trekking. The *gîtes* offer good basic accommodation – usually 4–6 bed dormitories with comfortable bunk beds – along with shared bathroom facilities. Guests take meals together, often at long trestle tables which make for a great atmosphere. Servings are unfailingly generous and some establishments even include wine at no extra charge. Prices start at around €15 for bed only, up to the €28–32 range for *demi pension* or half board, which means accommodation plus a full dinner then continental breakfast. This is generally a bowl of *café au lait*, *thé* or *chocolat* (milky coffee, tea or hot chocolate), served with *pain*,

21

Refuge de Ciottulu i Mori (Walk 8)

beurre and *confiture* (bread, butter and jam).

In addition, unless otherwise indicated in walk descriptions, all of the *gîtes d'étape* listed have self-cooking facilities *(coin cuisine)*, for which a small fee applies. A *panier-repas*, or packed picnic lunch, is another possibility if you ask ahead.

The only drawback occasionally encountered at the *gîtes d'étape* is late opening in the morning. Should you require *petit-déjeuner* (breakfast) before the official time, don't hesitate to ask, as some helpful places will lay out the food beforehand and leave you to make your own hot drink. In any case it's always good practice to settle your bill in the evening to save precious time the day after.

You'll need a sleeping sheet (though they can occasionally be rented) and your own towel – hot showers are always available. Book at least one day ahead (phone numbers are given in each walk description), more at peak holiday time. Most places are family-run affairs and they need due warning in order to be able to plan meals. A smattering of French will go a long way, especially when booking accommodation on the phone. (Italian won't go amiss either, as it is similar to the Corsican language itself.) Don't arrive too early as doors may not be opened until around 4pm. Some *gîtes* even offer to transport rucksacks for groups to villages ahead at a modest price.

Carry plentiful cash (euros) with you on the long-distance routes as the *gîtes* normally do not accept credit cards (not that they are widely accepted in the island's hotels or restaurants, for that matter). Eurocheques are not smiled upon either as they entail a hefty surcharge. ATMs are plentiful in tourist towns, mostly on the coast, but are rare as hen's teeth in the inland villages – as are banks. Be warned!

Before you set out it's also a good idea to purchase a prepaid phone card as the public telephones no longer accept coins. Most villages have a public phone, though a shop selling cards may be harder to find.

Modest hotels abound in tourist spots and have been listed where relevant to walks. After many nights in the communal hostels you may feel the need to treat yourself to some luxury.

Dotted along the high mountain paths are also refuge huts run by the PNRC, Corsica's Park Authority. They are open year-round, but manned only from June to October, when there is radio contact for emergencies. They charge a fee for dormitory-style accommodation, shared cooking (fully equipped kitchen) and washing facilities (WC and solar-heated shower), and wood-fuelled heating, but provide no meals or bedding. Basic food supplies are sometimes on sale. Refuges operate on a first-in first-served basis. Several are touched on during the itineraries in this guide and details given.

If you don't mind the extra weight, a tent and sleeping bag can spell a really cheap holiday. Wild camping is not permitted along any of the long-distance routes or in the realms of the National Park, but for a modest fee you can pitch in the immediate vicinity of both the *gîtes d'étape* and refuges, and have full use of the facilities. Corsica also has a multitude of camping grounds dotted around the island. Contact the local tourist offices listed for details.

FOOD AND DRINK

The island's cooking is basically French in the main tourist centres, but has retained its local flavour in the mountain villages and out-of-the-way places. On the coast you'll hopefully be offered the taste sensation *soupe de poisson* (fish soup), a delicate smooth seafood mixture served with croutons which are to be rubbed with fresh garlic and floated with a mayonnaise-mustard sauce, topped with grated cheese. *Civet de sanglier* or boar stew needs to be tasted at least once. The island's unusual cheeses are many and varied. Invariably tangy, either the richer ewe's milk *brebis,* smothered in dried maquis herbs, or the drier *fromage de chèvre* (goat) are must-try experiences. They may be served with fig conserve and even walnuts to cut the saltiness. Another cheese variety is soft white *brocciu,* flavoured with wild mint, which is melted in pastries or cannelloni.

The islanders have made some commendable adaptations to French paté, with the well-sung *paté de merle*

23

Most villages have drinking fountains

crèmes. One unusual speciality is *confiture d'arbousier*, jam made from the fruit of the strawberry tree, which grows abundantly in the island's maquis.

Tap water all over the island can be drunk safely (*potable*), unless you feel the urge to fork out for *eau minérale*. Some great beer is brewed on Corsica these days, otherwise there is no shortage of French brands. Wine on the other hand is either imported from the mainland or hails from the modest but interesting coastal vineyards. Wine growing was launched in the 1960s with the arrival of skilled labourers from Algeria, which had just won its independence from France. 'Appellation Contrôlée' is a guarantee of quality.

traditionally made with blackbirds – though supposedly outlawed nowadays. In the *charcuterie* range, *figatellu* or pork liver sausage should be on your list too.

Vegetarians will have a little trouble, as the majority of Corsican dishes are meat-based. However, try asking 'Est-ce qu'il ya quelque chose sans viande?' ('is there anything without meat?') or tell them 'Je suis végétarien' (*végétarienne* if female). *Crudités* will get you a plate of fresh vegetables; otherwise omelettes are regular fare. Corsican *soupe* is another good bet, invariably a hearty garlic-laden bean and vegetable number.

Sweet-toothers will enjoy the delicate dry *canistrelli* biscuits with aniseed. Many desserts incorporate *châtaignes* or chestnuts, the flour used effectively in concocting luscious

Food supply points for walkers on the long-distance routes are listed in the appropriate place in the route descriptions and shown on the summaries at the end of the book. Sometimes the *gîte d'étape* sells basics, however it's always a good idea to have durable reserves say of crackers, cheese and sweet biscuits to carry you over in case the awaited shops are closed. Many out-of-the-way villages without grocery stores are served by enterprising travelling bakers and greengrocers who announce their arrival in the main square with plenty of horn blowing. While they are unpredictable, they do mean a great opportunity to stock up on fresh fruit and bread, not to mention unfailingly luscious pastries.

The Tourist Offices (Office de Tourisme or Syndicat d'Initiative) in the principal towns are:

Ajaccio ☎ 04 95515303
Bastia ☎ 04 95559696
Bonifacio ☎ 04 95731188
Calvi ☎ 04 95651667
Corte ☎ 04 95462670
Porto ☎ 04 95261055
Porto-Vecchio ☎ 04 95700958
Propriano ☎ 04 95760149.

Other useful offices are listed under individual walks, distinguished by the symbol ①.

The international dialling code for France is 33, and is needed for calls from overseas.

The Parc Naturel Régional de Corse can be contacted at
2, Rue Casalonga
20000 Ajaccio
Corse
France
☎ 04 95517910
e-mail: infos@parc-naturel-corse.com
Its information-packed French-language web site is
www.parc-naturel-corse.com.

PLANT LIFE

Habitats on Corsica range from wind- and wave-lashed rocky coasts through to sun-baked plains, dense woodland and up to inhospitable snowbound mountain ranges, all home to well-adapted Mediterranean vegetation with everything from salt-resistant poppies to high-altitude crocus. But the majority of visitors to the island are struck by two things in particular: the pungent maquis and the noble Corsican pines.

The ever-present scrub cover (maquis) spells subtle background scents that blend rosemary with endemic thyme, fennel, myrtle and much else besides. It leaves a lasting impression on all visitors, literary and non-literary figures alike. For Paul Theroux (1995) 'It smells like a barrel of potpourri, it is like holding a bar of expensive soap to your nose, it is Corsica's own Vap-o-Rub. The Corsican *maquis* is strong enough to clear your lungs and cure your cold.' Guy de Maupassant (1881) noted

Clump of broom in rock cranny

that it made the air heavy, while for Dorothy Carrington, steaming towards the island for the very first time, 'This is the scent of all Corsica: bitter-sweet, akin to incense, heady, almost, as an anaesthetic after rain... it is a perpetual and potent enchantment'.

The hardy, woody maquis shrubs that thrive on sun-baked earth have hidden generations of bandits, and there is even a historical record of Roman soldiers hopelessly losing their way. Predominant is the cistus or rock rose, a straggly bush with small leathery blooms in pastel colours of mauve, pink and white. A curious parasite plant, *Cytinus hypocistis*, often grows at its base, its attractive yellow–red sheath resembling a mushroom. Another maquis standard is the strawberry tree, a type of arbutus. This evergreen is easily identified by its ball-like fruit reminiscent of strawberries in appearance, though not exactly in taste, and glossy leaves that resemble laurel. A member of the heather family, it is known in Corsica as a symbol of loyalty: according to legend the shrub hid Christ when fleeing from his enemies. However, the traitorous heather did not hesitate to give him away and he was captured. The charitable strawberry tree was blessed with fruit, while the heather was condemned to flower without ever producing fruit. Its woody stem, however, is prized for pipe-making.

Other notables are the widespread shady evergreen holm oak, with tiny glossy leaves and small acorns, as well as the dark-green-leaved lentisc with clusters of red berries. The bright myrtle shrub has delicate blooms like hawthorn, and its wood is still used for basketmaking.

Pretty rock roses

Cytinus hypocistis, *parasite on rock rose shrub*

At a similar low–medium altitude vegetation band are native Mediterranean cork oaks. Still important to the island's economy, they are a common sight half stripped of their bark, leaving the bare trunk blushing bright red in its exposed state. The tough covering is non-flammable, a natural protection from summer bush fires.

Another curiosity is the Indian bead tree, planted in villages. It features lilac blossoms and orange woody ball fruits, which gave it its name.

One landmark tree for Corsica is the chestnut. Under Genoese domination in the mid-16th century they became the island's mainstay. Later, a grand total of 35,000 hectares under cultivation was recorded in the 1800s, though it was destined to decline with the first blight in the early 1900s. A mere 4000 hectares are productive nowadays. The nuts were dried slowly in the typical double-floored *séchoir* huts over a fire burning day and night. They were later milled for flour.

Many of Corsica's mountains have their lower 800–1800m zones cloaked in magnificent forests of endemic Corsica or laricio pine modelled into weird sculptures by wind action on exposed passes. Reaching up to a maximum of 40m in height they account for a good 50,000 hectares, including the Aïtone, Vizzavona and Bavella forests, and were highly prized by the Romans as masts for their galleys. Easily confused with the maritime variety, the Corsican pine has short rounded cones and dark bark with sizeable rough patches. The maritime, in contrast, features deeply fissured bark, often crimson, while its cones are large and pointed.

In terms of flowers, April is the best time for a visit on the coastal belt, though this will be postponed if the spring rain is late in coming.

Down at sea level many beaches are scattered with curious soft spongy

Old chestnut trees reach remarkable dimensions

brown balls, remnants of a flowering seaweed *Posidonia oceanica* ('king of the sea'). As they detach from the plant and die, the broad fronds are broken up by the waves, which then roll them up and wash them onto the coast. They are quite effective for removing tar stains, an unlikely predicament. Other seaside habitués include the showy yellow horned poppy, with blue-grey leaves, and the widespread crimson Hottentot fig, a native of South Africa as the name suggests.

Not far away is the inland habitat of highly perfumed French lavender, its tasselled head distinguishing it from the better-known variety cultivated commercially. The divine scent of an astonishing variety of yellow broom is another constant on Corsica. More perfume comes from sweet honeysuckle draped over walls and other shrubs. It comes in a deep red version as well as the more common creamy gold. An eye-catcher on otherwise bare rock surfaces is vivid purple and pink stonecrop.

Prickly pear cactus or the Barbary fig keeps a low profile, producing bright papery flowers in spring, followed by edible fruit for anyone patient enough to peel off the insidious spiky needles. Christopher Columbus is believed to have introduced it to the Mediterranean from South America. In the past the leaves were applied to wounds to stop bleeding. Giant fennel or ferula is a common sight towering over arid hillsides. Its tall dried stalks were once crafted into modest furniture and walking sticks, as well as serving as reliable, slow-burning torches. A sure sign of exhausted over-grazed terrain is the presence of the asphodel, tall lily-like plant with white flowers. The Greeks called it the 'flower of death', but in Corsica it was known as the 'poor people's bread', as the bulb, rich in starch, was eaten widely until the introduction of the potato in the late 1700s. The dried plant is still used in rituals, and is widely held to be a powerful protector as well as an effective cure for warts.

Higher up, wet zones around mountain streams often feature pretty lilac butterwort, their sticky leaves ready to trap insects. There's also the odd orchid, mainly the modest serapias, better known as the tongue orchid, rather nondescript burgundy-cream with pointy elongated petals. A more striking orchid look-alike is the violet-green thick-stemmed limodore. Other notable wood-dwellers include pretty crimson-purple cyclamens and the endemic toxic Corsican hellebore, with attractive drooping lime green flowers. Its broad leaves were used by shepherds to keep their cheeses fresh, while the roots produced a valuable disinfectant for livestock.

Lastly, two glorious showy flowers found in mountainous zones: a striking white lily similar to amaryllis and sea daffodil, the *Pancratium illyricum*, is endemic to both Corsica and Sardinia and is commonly encountered. Much rarer in the springtime are the bright pink peonies that grow wild on the edge of forests.

Flowers of the Mediterranean by Oleg Polunin and Anthony Huxley (Chatto & Windus, 1987) makes a valuable and enjoyable companion.

WILDLIFE

Thick woodland and impenetrable maquis do not facilitate observation of wild animals in Corsica, nor does the widespread hunting! Quiet walkers in the mountainous regions can hope for at least a glimpse of the 'king of the island', the stocky goat-like mouflon recognisable by its showy curling horns. With a history stretching back 8000 years, this native of Corsica and neighbouring Sardinia has reportedly become shy in the extreme in the face of species-threatening poaching. Protected herds of several hundred mouflon survive in reserves in the Asco and Bavella areas and small groups have been reported in the seafront Scandola promontory.

Much more successful is the introduced well-adapted boar (*sanglier*), their numbers around the 30,000 mark. Along with pigs normally left free by their owners, they roam medium-altitude woodland in search of edible roots, leaving a trail of devastation in their wake. Not even the avid hunters seem able to dent the population. Again these are timid creatures, and the closest most visitors ever get to an actual boar is a hide left by hunters to dry on a fence. Both boar and pig are part and parcel of Corsican life –

Foraging pigs

and cooking. In the legendary past they even organised a revolution, led by the talking specimen Porcafonu from Calenzana, who conducted discussions with the Almighty for more humane treatment for the hoofers.

Another 'success' story concerns small red deer. After they were shot to extinction in the 1960s, park authorities combined forces with hunters' groups to reintroduce eight deer from Sardinia in 1985. This number rose to 103 in a mere three years, and they have since been released to fend for themselves near Quenza in the Bavella region.

In terms of reptiles Corsica does not have any life-endangering snakes, vipers being totally absent. On the other hand walkers have a good chance of encountering harmless green-grey and black snakes which will not hesitate to hiss fiercely, a strategy to give them time to slither away to safety. Other notables on the ground are the ubiquitous darting lizards.

Last but not least, the enterprising dung beetles are entitled to a mention. Key creatures on an island where livestock is an essential part of the economy, they are encountered on pathways in bands industriously dispatching cow pats, often engaged in clown-like bickering.

The best news relates to birdlife. Magnificent birds of prey such as splendid rust-red kites with marked forked tails can be seen gliding in couples surveying open mountainsides for small animals. The woods are alive with myriad finches, woodpeckers and the dainty tree creeper spiralling its way up tree trunks in search of burrowing insects to feed its offspring concealed in a crack in the bark. The curious hoopoe swoops and dips over light shrub emitting its characteristic 'hoo hoo' call (hence the name), its distinctive black–white wings contrasting with its warm orange-nut-coloured body.

Eight couples of lammergeier (bearded vulture) are known to breed on Corsica in high spots such as the Bavella massif. Known locally as the Altore ('dweller of high places'), the imposing bird has a wing span up to 2.7m. It lives on carrion and is famous for its original practice of dropping bones from a great height to crack them on rocks. Despite local hearsay and shepherd's tales, it does not prey on lambs, in contrast to the golden eagle, only a little smaller in size. Thirty couples of eagles thrive along the central mountain chain as well as the easternmost Castagniccia. The eagle has a wedge-shaped tail whereas the lammergeier can be distinguished by its more slender elongated tail.

Acrobatic swifts and martins swooping and screeching overhead are a distinctive sight in the mountainous villages during the warm summer months. As the typical stone houses have unusually narrow eaves with no overhang suitable for nests, the birds often make do with cracks in the masonry walls.

FURTHER READING

Top of the list is *Asterix in Corsica* by R. Goscinny and A. Uderzo (1973, out of print), which captures the island's nature in a delightfully irreverent manner. A close second is *Granite Island: A Portrait of Corsica* (Penguin 1971), a serious read verging on gripping, this is Dorothy Carrington's passionate and detailed account of late 1940s Corsica set against a web of spirits. Those with access to an antique book store should search out Edward Lear's *Journal of a Landscape Painter in Corsica* (1870) and either of James Boswell's travel journals dating back to the late 1700s. Latter-day traveller Paul Theroux also passed through, as recounted in his very readable *The Pillars of Hercules: A Grand Tour of the Mediterranean* (Penguin 1995).

French readers should look out for the mesmerising short stories by Guy de Maupassant including *Un bandit corse* (1882), *Histoire corse* (1881) and *La Patrie de Colomba* (1880). There's also fascinating reading in *Contes et Légendes de l'île de Corse* by Gabriel Xavier Culioli (Éditions DCL 1998) and Claire Tiévant and Lucie Desideri's *Almanach de la mémoire et des coutumes: Corse* (Albin Michel 1986).

Beach and jetties at Girolata (Walk 3/Mare e Monti)

LONG-DISTANCE WALKS

Mare e Monti: Calenzana to Cargèse

Walking time	48hr 45min – 10 days
Distance	124.4km/77.1 miles
Difficulty	Grade 2
Maps	IGN 1:25,000 sheets 4149OT, 4159OT, 4151OT
Start	Calenzana
Finish	Cargèse

The longest-standing and easily the most wonderful long-distance route in Corsica, the Mare e Monti holds true to its name and provides a roller coaster of treats ranging from breathtaking coastline with blue sea and beaches to some awe-inspiring mountainous land-scapes. It effects a huge 'S' as it heads southwards, ducking in and out of the reliefs parallel to Corsica's rugged west coast. The many and varied highlights include the Forest of Bonifatu, the Fango river gorge, the isolated fishing village of Girolata, the Golfe de Porto and the Spelunca gorge, along with days and days of wandering through memorable maquis impregnated with the scents of the Mediterranean and unbelievable masses of wild flowers.

The Mare e Monti is sometimes referred to as Tra Mare e Monti, abbreviated as TMM on signposts. Carry plenty of drinking water every day – although numerous watercourses are encountered, they are not necessarily reliable in terms of either quality or quantity. Another must is swimming gear for the rock pools, rivers and sea.

The route is theoretically feasible all year round in terms of terrain and weather, however in terms of accommodation, only a handful of the establishments stay open during winter. The concluding two days are

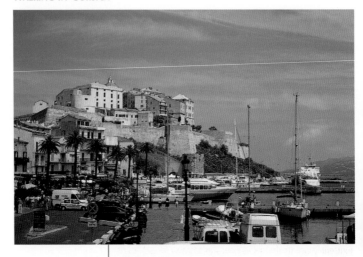

Calvi with its citadel and port

shared with the Mare-Mare Nord route, and it is therefore a good idea to pre-book accommodation. Should the entire 10-day walk be too long in terms of time, it can be shortened by either compressing a couple of days (if you're fit), or doing it in shorter chunks as nearly all the villages touched on have bus services. A tricky task is to choose the 'best' part of the route for people short of time – a hazarded suggestion would be the Bonifatu–Curzu or the Serriera–Evisa legs. The walk can also be lengthened by slotting into the Mare-Mare Nord route at Evisa and branching eastwards towards the island's centre and Corte.

En route to the start, everyone passes through Calvi ① 04 95651667. This charming seaside town with a picturesque Genoese citadel (now occupied by the French Foreign Legion) is cleverly placed on a magnificent promontory, overlooking a colourful leisure port alongside a divine white sand beach. A curious item of historic trivia: in the late 1700s during a siege of the citadel by the English under Horatio Nelson, the great man won the battle but sustained serious injury to his right eye. A further if somewhat dubious claim to fame is the town's profession to be the birthplace of Christopher Columbus! Calvi has shops galore, as well as restaurants and accommodation for all pockets, including the centrally located hostel BVJ Corsotel ☎ 04 95651415, open April–October.

Access: The closest town to the start point is Calvi, a handy transport hub. The island's train comes this far via the Ponte-Leccia junction, as do coaches from Bastia and several ferries from the French mainland in summer. The walk start itself, at Calenzana, 12km inland (south-east of Calvi on the D151), is served by a twice-daily bus from Calvi's railway station, but only during midsummer. At other times there's a school bus. Failing that either try hitching or get a group together and hire a taxi – the GR20 commences here too, so trekkers are plentiful.

Villages encountered en route can be used as exit/entry points thanks to buses as follows. Tuarelli has a school-day bus to Galéria, which in turn is served by a school run and midsummer link with Calvi. Curzu and Serriera are on the May–October line between Porto and Calvi. Further on, from Ota you can reach Porto then Cargèse all year. Evisa and Marignana on the other hand have year-round links with Ajaccio, and Evisa is linked summer-only with Corte. The novel (and only!) way to leave the isolated fishing hamlet of Girolata is by boat to Porto or Calvi. At the trail's conclusion, Cargèse, there are always coaches for the 51km south to the island's capital, Ajaccio, as well as services north back towards the start.

DAY 1: CALENZANA TO BONIFATU
(total 4hr, 11.3km/7 miles, ascent/descent 560m/300m) ▶

Calenzana (275m) – *gîte d'étape* and camping ground (5min on foot before Calenzana) ☎ 04 95627713, sleeps 30, open April–October, no meals. Shops and restaurants in the village proper, also a hotel, Bel Horizon ☎ 04 95627172. Apart from screeching swooping swifts, it is a quiet spot these days, in contrast

A wonderful start to the Mare e Monti, this stage through the Balagne region, 'the garden of Corsica', takes you out of the agricultural flats backing the coast and straight up to a panoramic ridge and wild rocky reliefs. It then heads into the beautiful Bonifatu forest where a cosy hotel-cum-gîte d'étape is ensconced.

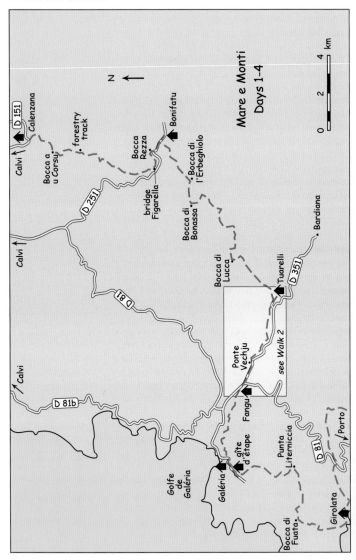

Mare e Monti
Days 1-4

to its reputed past as a hot bed of gangsters according to Ian Fleming.

Fill up your water bottle at the cool fountain in the main street close to the church, then turn right uphill for the Mare e Monti, in common with the GR20 for the time being. Plentiful waymarks lead out of the south-east edge of Calenzana and up to a paved path that winds and climbs steadily south-southwest through masses of heady herbs and flowers with the odd shady patch. Sheep tracks criss-cross the slopes and bright broom has colonised abandoned terracing beneath curious weathered rock formations. At a junction where the GR20 heads off on its own course, you keep right to follow orange paint splashes to the nearby scenic ample grassy saddle of

1hr – Bocca a u Corsu (581m). Due south now the path plunges down a wild dry hillside carpeted with scented broom and rock roses. Two stream crossings later it emerges at a bend to join a **forestry track** (415m). Keep straight on in imperceptible ascent following the contour line. While the going is a little monotonous, it gives you time to admire the accompanying blooms of the maquis shrubs, including the strawberry tree. These are the reforested realms of the Forêt de Sambuccu. Bearing east below prominent Punta Scaffa you head downhill past striking granite formations with views up to the peaks crowning the Cirque de Bonifatu, and to

2hr – bridge over the Figarella (360m). A boulder-choked watercourse with good spots for a cooling dip. After the crossing, the path (left) clambers over a dry rocky bed then hugs the stream. A short detour to a stunning natural pool, complete with its own cascade, is followed by a prominent rock overhang sheltering Corsican lilies and cyclamen. Then the path turns right in zigzags to emerge at the road and

Near the bridge over the Figarella

45min – Bocca Rezza (510m). With an inspiring back-drop of pink granite mountains inland, turn left on the D251 through shady wood for the remaining stroll to

15min – Bonifatu (535m). Set amidst towering pines and boasting a restful rose-draped terrace, Auberge de la Fôret (☎ 04 95650998, sleeps 32, open April–October) doubles as hotel and *gîte d'étape* and serves delicious hearty cuisine. No self-catering. The only drawback is getting early breakfast, as the staff go home to the coast of an evening and you may have to wait.

A day could profitably be spent here exploring the valley leading to Refuge Carozzu and a suspension bridge – ask at the Auberge for details.

DAY 2: BONIFATU TO TUARELLI

A tiring but rewarding traverse of the wild Forêt de Bonifatu terminating at an idyllically located riverside hostel.

(total 5hr 30min, 16.5km/10.2 miles, ascent/descent 655m/1100m)

Backtrack a short distance down the **D251** to a stone bridge and huge signpost for the Mare e Monti. The clear path starts climbing in a southwesterly direction through beautiful shady forest of pine mixed with turkey oak. Underfoot amidst moss are pretty cyclamens and oversized Corsican hellebore, not to mention chaotic boar scratchings. Across the torrent are evocative ruins of the so-called **Chalet Prince Pierre** (the son of Bonaparte's brother Lucien). Soon afterwards is a fine **lookout** over lightly wooded red granite mountainsides with the meanders of the Figarella river.

A cover of tree heather and maritime pines with fissured bark dominate on the ensuing zigzagging slog that finally concludes the 700m climb at

2hr – Bocca di l'Erbeghiolo (1200m). Once you've got your breath back there are views all the way back to Calvi to be enjoyed. The path continues left (west) in descent to

15min – Bocca di Bonassa (1153m), which marks a surprisingly abrupt departure from the forest and you are surrounded by the fragrances of the maquis. Plunging views open up southwest. The descent path due south is all but suffocated by masses of lavender and Corsican hellebore for the initial dry tract, however light wood reappears as a constant companion and even the odd chestnut tree. You bear southwest and traverse countless streams in varying states of dryness, and pass round a rearing rock head outcrop. There are occasional views despite the dense wood cover. The next landmark is the marked saddle

2hr 10min – Bocca di Lucca (575m). Slow but sure descent through shoulder-high rock roses and juniper along with asphodels leads down to a quiet road. Turn sharp left parallel to the bank of the Fango river where you can collapse at

1hr 5min – Tuarelli (90m). Camping ground and *gîte* ☎ 04 95620175, mobile ☎ 06 10773192, sleeps 24, open April–October, no cooking facilities. Marvellous soups and stews prepared by friendly staff. But before dinner two activities are compulsory: an invigorating swim in the incredibly transparent pools of the Fango river, followed by a cool beer on the veranda in the shade of olive trees looking inland to the Paglia Orba. School-day bus from the nearby village.

DAY 3: TUARELLI TO GALÉRIA
(total 3hr 50min, 10.8km/6.7 miles, ascent/descent 230m/290m)

Follow the lane from the *gîte* back along the river to a bridge over a stunning gorge, but turn right without crossing it. A path quickly breaks off left to follow the river through waist-high rock roses and myrtle bushes. There are some superb swimming spots, and lovely views of the orange-red smooth porphyry rock-base the water has patiently moulded. Soon in sight is the

You are led back to the coast today, and – in view of the relatively short distance to be covered – can enjoy the lovely natural rock pools along the course of the crystal-clear Fango, whose name funnily enough means mud!

1hr 15min – Ponte Vechju (46m). Elegantly arched Genoese bridge, stunningly restored to its former glory. Your last chance for a dip – before the sea. Cross the bridge to a restaurant and pick up the D351 (right) northwest towards the coast. 1.5km along past a drinking fountain and farm properties is a junction where you keep right for

20min – Fangu (29m). Bus, snack bars and family-run Hotel a Farera (or Chez Zeze) ☎ 04 95620187. B&B La Casaloha ☎ 04 95344695.

A short way along the D81, immediately after a minor bridge, the Mare e Monti turns off left at a restaurant sign to climb into a veritable canopy of tree heather above the road, essentially northwest. A lengthy stretch of dry scratchy scrub sees you through to a sizeable **water tank** and rough track. Maintaining the same direction a path resumes for gentle ups and downs and the odd watercourse, not to mention cows.

You eventually climb past an abandoned shepherd's hut encircled by huge fennel plants. A **180m col** is gained overlooking the enticing coast and the delta of the Fango river. Flanking an old stone wall the path descends easily to the seaside village of

2hr – Galéria (40m). Shops, ice creams, bus, restaurants and modest hotels including centrally sited L'Auberge ☎ 04 95620015. Decent if gravely beach. Evocative cemetery with monumental family tombs silhouetted on the seafront. 4km out of town is the summer-only ① 04 95620227.

Past the post office and phone boxes, follow signs southwest for Calca along the quiet country road to the scatter of farms and

15min – gîte d'étape (30m) in a rural relaxed atmosphere. The spotless spacious L'Étape Marine ☎ 04 95620046, sleeps 36, open March to November, no cooking facilities, is a great place run by two welcoming Corsican sisters from Marseille, though early breakfast is a sticky issue. Camping ground too.

DAY 4: GALÉRIA TO GIROLATA
(total 5hr, 11.8km/7.3 miles, ascent/descent 770m/800m)

From Calca and the *gîte* turn left (southwest) along the road. After a bridge you are pointed left into the bush to penetrate a lovely wild valley headed by red rock crests. Shaded by oaks and chestnut, the path goes back and forth across a stream and passes a **small dam**. Heaps of old stone walls are encountered, overgrown with lentisc and rock roses, whose roots host an attractive red-yellow parasite akin to a mushroom.

At a large cairn there are lovely views back down over Galéria and a succession of headlands. The path winds up a little higher to a ridge where you catch sight of the serpentine Calvi–Porto road and look inland to jagged rows of crests. Bear right amid thick cistus bushes to soon reach a prominent evergreen oak and signed junction

2hr 30min – Punta Literniccia (778m). Wonderful outlook down to the bay where the Girolata hamlet nestles, then over to Capo Senino and even Capu Rossu beyond. Here a Mare e Monti short-cut (bypassing Girolata)

One of the top days, this sees you cross the scenic wooded ridge separating the Golfe de Galéria from the glorious Golfe de Girolata and drop in to an isolated fishing settlement accessible exclusively by sea or footpath. There's a very brief, averagely exposed passage in the middle section, slippery in the wet.

breaks off south for the road at Col de Palmarella before picking up the official path for Curzu.

Following the broad crest, the path bears west with plenty of openings in the light wood cover for constantly improving views. Shrubs have been sculpted into bonsai shapes by the combined effect of livestock nibbling and wind action. A sizeable **cairn** doubles as a marvellous viewpoint that includes the distinctive shape of Paglia Orba east-southeast. Then the ridge narrows considerably, obliging you to a short clamber over exposed rock. The next landmark consists of antennae and a small **weather station**.

The descent begins easily through thickets of rock roses, overlooking the warm red rocks of the Scandola promontory and tortuous coastline with myriad inlets. An oblique descent (right) leads to a semi-circle of stones on the ample saddle

1hr 15min – Bocca di Fuata (458m). West is the wild headland belonging to the protected Scandola Reserve. The path drops easily due south and follows a wide ravine down to sea level. A lovely path turns left for the delightful last leg coasting over divine green-blue waters towards the Genoese watchtower and haven of

1hr 15min – Girolata. The sleepy fishing settlement has a lively summertime population as restaurants open up and families return, whereas in winter the figure oscillates between one and ten. Boats will take passengers to Porto and Calvi as well as on trips around the Scandola promontory, as access by land is strictly banned. In terms of facilities, there's a modest grocery store and two welcoming *gîtes d'étape*: set just above the bay is Le Cormoran Voyageur ☎ 04 95201555, sleeps 20, open April to end September, no kitchen facilities but freshly caught fish and home-made jam are served. Otherwise a lovely beachfront restaurant provides rustic timber huts for its guests – La Cabane du Berger ☎ 04 95201698, sleeps 30, open April to end September.

DAY 5: GIROLATA TO CURZU

(total 6hr, 13.6km/8.4 miles, ascent/descent 890m/600m)

Head along the eucalpyt-backed shingle beach with its jetties. At the far end, with a stream surrounded by a mass of yellow horned poppies, a path leads uphill past a tiny cemetery. Bearing east, it climbs over slabs alongside a dry-stone wall amidst shady shrubs to a signpost and

45min – col (150m). The variant branches off here. Keep left for the steady ascent northeast through colourful rock roses, taking your time to reach the road

1hr 10min – D81 (352m). Keeping an eye out for traffic on this narrow stretch, turn right along the tarmac until you are pointed up left and the path resumes (northeast). Ascending rocky sand-based terrain with the pleasant scent of ever-present maquis shrubs, the views improve with every step. On reaching **Punta di u Munditoghju** (640m) the path changes direction markedly and you bear right (east). Some level terrain at last leads to the foot of prominent Punta di u Tartavellu (only a short distance from Tuarelli as the crow flies). Here you bear right (south) to the next landmark, **Bocca Ascensu** (742m). More ascent follows, but Punta Salisei is thankfully detoured and you embark southwest on the marvellously panoramic Crête de Salisei. This culminates in stunning

3hr – Capu di Curzu (852m), the day's record in terms of height, not to mention the start of the descent at last! You drop quickly to a

15min – signposted col (750m), where the shorter variant via Bocca a Croce joins up.

Variant: from the 150m col, keep right (southeast) downhill for Tuara beach, where you may encounter the odd cow. A broad shady way then climbs steadily southwards past a drinking fountain and

A weary climb looping along a succession of elevated rugged ridges, with effort amply recompensed by the sweeping views over the spectacular coastline. It all comes to a fitting conclusion at a well-reputed gîte-cum-restaurant. A viable shorter variant is given below.

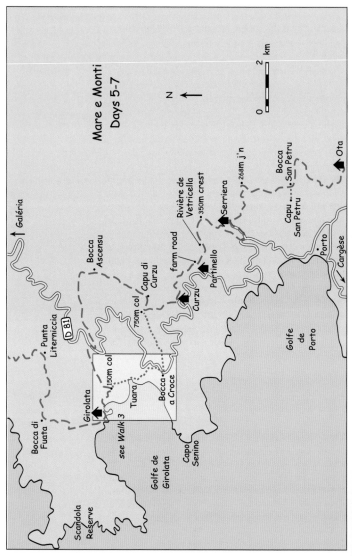

Mare e Monti
Days 5-7

emerges on the D81 at the snack bar at Bocca a Croce (269m, 1hr). You can always bail out here thanks to the Porto–Calvi bus.

Straight across the road clamber up the bank to a hut with a radio aerial, where you'll find markers pointing straight up (east-northeast). A steep haul ensues to a panoramic crest flanking Capu di Linu, quickly followed by a 750m col below Capu di Corzu, where the main route is joined (1hr 30min from Bocca a Croce). This variant makes a saving of about 2hr.

The last leg to the village entails more tiring stony terrain and age-old olive trees. On the upper outskirts at the first houses, keep right at a signed junction for a succession of steps and laneways past old stone ovens to a drinking fountain and the D81 once more. Keep right for rather nondescript

50min – Curzu (290m). The Calvi–Porto bus can picked up here. Some groceries available. Well-equipped *gîte* with an excellent reputation for traditional Corsican catering ☎ 04 95273170, sleeps 35, open April–October.

DAY 6: CURZU TO SERRIERA
(total 3hr 15min, 7.9km/4.9 miles, ascent/descent 430m/690m)

Climb back up past the drinking fountain the way you arrived. Just below the last house turn right (southeast) on a goat track along overgrown terraces. Waymarking is constant but the going is particularly thorny – be warned! You coast above the cemetery and make your way past red rock outcrops and thickets of strawberry trees to a shoulder (370m). Not far downhill is a signpost and

1hr 15min – farm road (280m).

A straightforward if somewhat uninteresting traverse of hills clad in scratchy maquis and scrubby pastureland, and ending at an attractive *gîte*.

By turning right, in 30min you can **detour** to the cluster of houses that goes by the name of Partinello. On the panoramic verge of the D81, it has a café, restaurant and hotel Aria Marina ☎ 04 95273033, open May– September.

◀ Continue straight across the unsealed road down past a paddock, keeping an eye out for faint paint splashes. These indicate a steepish descent beneath turkey oaks and cool undergrowth to the

20min – Rivière de Vetricella (66m), forded easily thanks to large stepping stones. You climb out of the river valley to a

1hr – 350m crest, and clearing with huge juniper bushes, asphodels and a signpost. Visible just off the path are the photogenic abandoned stone houses of Pinedu.

On a wider older way you bear south-southwest between grazing fields (ignore misleading waymarks that induce you to leave the old lane). You eventually emerge on the D81. It's a sharp left to the crossroads (bus service) and the turn-off left up a green river valley. Close at hand is a decent hotel with a swimming pool, Cabanaccia ☎ 04 95261446, open April to October. A further 10min uphill is

Grocery shop at Serriera

40min – Serriera (30m). It boasts a small grocery store, drinking fountain and ubiquitous phone box near the Mairie. A short stroll on is an old building housing the village olive press, recently converted into the *gîte* L'Alivi ☎ 04 95104933, mobile 06 17559051, sleeps 32, open year-round, no self-catering.

DAY 7: SERRIERA TO OTA
(total 5hr 40min, 10.8km/6.7 miles, ascent/descent 900m/610m)

From the village of **Serriera** (30m), opposite the shop, take the lane down to the river's edge to cross the concrete footbridge. You join a wide dirt forestry track (left) climbing east for some 2km. At a **268m junction** a clear path forks off right into shady wood, where ring clearings once used by charcoal burners are encountered. An outcrop overlooks Serriera and the surrounding wild hills, then the climb resumes amidst pretty white ball blossoms of tree heather and lavender. Further up, the appearance of pines means you've almost completed the ascent to a broad crest clad in fresh green chestnut at

After a lengthy taxing climb comes the reward in the shape of brilliant views, a magnificent pine forest and a wild and wonderful ravine down to a beautifully located hospitable village.

2hr 40min – Bocca San Petru (900m). Recommended detour (see below) to a superb lookout, not to mention perfect picnic spot.

Side trip to Capu San Petru (30min return)
Turn right for the clear level path due west along the narrowing crest thick with asphodels and bracken. You clamber the last easy metres to rock perches on Capu San Petru (914m), a breathtaking belvedere over the Golfe de Porto all the way from Capu Rossu to Scandola. Also south across the valley are the eye-catching granite columns on Capu d'Ortu. Return the same way to Bocca San Petru.

A wide path proceeds east-southeast alternating towering maritime pines with sweet chestnut and even the rare peony. After a ruined hut for drying chestnuts, a head of valley is rounded and the long descent commences southwards. Lookout points survey the coast, while closer at hand are massive rugged walls of deep red porphyry as you follow the magnificent Vitrone ravine. The stream is crossed several times then followed closely in a series of knee-jarring steps dwarfed by oppressive cliffs.

Finally out of the ravine, the path swerves left (south then southeast) past a little waterfall, a fairly level stretch providing respite from the previous steepness. Accompanied by a surprising range of orchids you gain a panoramic saddle, then embark on the last leg due east, with never-ending ups and downs to

3hr – Ota (320m). The pretty village swarming with swifts seems to function exclusively in terms of the multitudinous walkers attracted by the Spelunca gorge. Draped in honeysuckle creepers and adorned with fragrant lime trees, it looks over to impressive Capu d'Ortu. There's a good bus service and food supplies, as well as

The village of Ota surrounded by woods and mountains

two popular *gîtes d'étape*: Chez Marie ☎ 04 95261137, sleeps 30, open year-round, and Chez Félix ☎ 04 95261292, sleeps 50, open year-round.

DAY 8: OTA TO MARIGNANA
(total 5hr, 11.7km/7.3 miles, ascent/descent 650m/260m)

After Chez Félix restaurant, head downhill (east) via lanes through terraces of olives and citrus for the gentle descent to the Rivière de Porto and the

40min – Pont Génois (200m) (also known as Ponte Vecchiu or Vechju). Reputedly the most beautiful restored 15th-century bridge of its kind on the island. Over the bridge the path turns left along the river bank past a playing field to a **road bridge** at the confluence of two watercourses. A delightful path rambles up the right bank of the Aïtone amidst bright masses of wild flowers. The rock walls of the gorge become taller as you approach through dense vegetation to what is left of

40min – Pont de Zaglia (280m). Side paths lead off along the converging watercourses to a good selection of water holes for a swim and relax, not a bad idea in view of the imminent stiff climb.

Continuing eastwards, the gorge is left behind as you puff up tight switchbacks edged by old stone walls beneath evergreen oaks and pines. The path finally levels out as you reach the cemetery and the D84, which is followed a short way to scenic

2hr 10min – Evisa (850m). Briefly uphill is Hotel U Pozzu ☎ 04 95262289, open April–October; otherwise turn down after the bakery and grocery store, then left for the good family-run *gîte* ☎ 04 95262188, sleeps 37, open April to mid-October. A relaxing day-trip is suggested to the renowned rock pools on the Aïtone – see Walk 7. Slotting into the Mare-Mare Nord is also feasible here. Buses to Ajaccio and the coast.

A landmark stage negotiating the lovely Spelunca gorge featuring elegant Genoese bridges. Allow extra time for swimming. If it fits in with your plans, make your overnight stay at Evisa, as accommodation and services there are preferable to those at Marignana. In either case, book ahead as both villages are used by walkers on the Mare-Mare Nord – this applies to all remaining accommodation on this route.

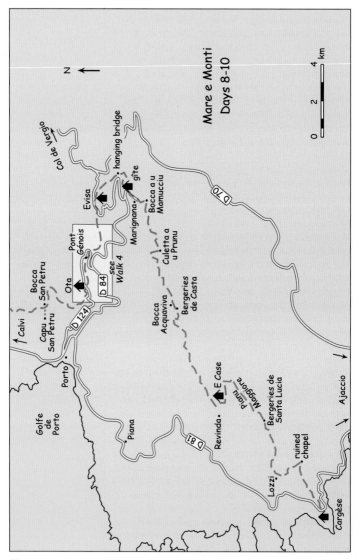

Mare e Monti
Days 8-10

From the *gîte d'étape* proceed southeast along the road. On a corner just as the houses finish, branch off right for the descent via rough lanes to a stream crossing. An old wall is followed before a steep drop to the Tavulella and a **40min – hanging bridge (635m).** The watercourse is crossed three more times, then a narrow path leads up to the abandoned hamlet of **U Tassu** (700m). A level stretch through chestnut woods brings you out at the road and

50min – Marignana gîte d'étape (700m) (or Ustaria di a Rota) ☎ 04 95262121, sleeps 40, always open. Groceries on sale. A further 10min up the road is the village proper, with buses to Ajaccio.

DAY 9: MARIGNANA TO E CASE
(total 6hr, 17km/10.6 miles, ascent/descent 825m/930m)

Head up the road past the cemetery to

10min – Marignana (715m). At the church turn left up the cobbled streets to woodland teeming with foraging pigs. Past the playing ground is a cross at

30min – Bocca a u Mamucciu (824m). A Mare-Mare Nord variant branches off southeast.

Sharp right a rough lane climbs to a crest, where you need to keep your eyes skinned for faint paint splashes for the path (left) across rock slabs into a chestnut copse. Aromatic flowered maquis soon takes over and a level old mule track heads west-southwest with great views all the way to the coast. At a minor pass **Culetta a u Prunu** (970m), the path narrows and turns down decidedly right (north) into chestnut woods and past a *séchoir* hut once used for drying the nuts. Some remarkably gnarled trees are encountered, testifying to their erstwhile importance for the local economy.

A couple of streams are crossed before you climb a dramatic red cleft valley and resume a southwest direction. Paved tracts of an old winding track appear from

Another long day with plenty of ups and downs across wild rocky valleys miles from anywhere. Wild flowers feature high on the list of attractions.

time to time, leading through a marvellous extended garden of rock roses, lilies and lavender to name but a few. A gradual ascent across rougher scrubby terrain concludes at the ample panoramic saddle

2hr 30min – Bocca Acquaviva (1102m), shaded by Capu e Macenue. Coasting west at first through overgrazed pasture past signs for a 'source' (spring), you drop to the circular stone enclosures of the abandoned Bergeries de Casta. Follow cairns down the wide crest to an outcrop at 960m, where tight zigzags plunge you into the thickly wooded valley of Rognia with its many streams. A long, easy wander southwest through shady wood of strawberry trees and evergreen oak leads past the signed fork (right) for the hamlet of Revinda. A short further way on (southeast) you reach the isolated *gîte d'étape* of

Converted farmhouse, now the gîte d'étape E Case

2hr 50min – E Case (605m) ☎ 04 95264819 (guardian's house at Revinda) or mobile ☎ 06 82499565, sleeps 22, open April–October, booking recommended. Wonderfully

situated overlooking the coast and Golfe de Chiuni, this simple family-run stone farmhouse extends a warm welcome to weary walkers. Meals are served *al fresco* and supplies come in courtesy of the mule. Don't expect any mod cons though.

DAY 10: E CASE TO CARGÈSE
(total 4hr 30min, 13km/8 miles, ascent/descent 400m/910m)

Head off southeast into shoulder-high maquis across a gurgling stream then continue in gradual ascent through lilies galore, then gigantic strawberry trees, to the rocky crests of **Pianu Maggiore**, culminating at 650m. There are views back to Revinda, not to mention the approaching promising coast.

After an outcrop (471m), turn sharp left following a fence for a scrambly drop through dry scrub alongside paddocks. This finally terminates at a dirt track at

1hr 40min – Bergeries de Santa Lucia (220m). Follow the lane that loops down past a fork to cross the Esigna watercourse (about 190m) and stay on it for a matter of kilometres west. After a succession of stream crossings you reach a signed junction for Lozzi, but fork left to ford the watercourse (70m).

Waymarking needs following carefully for the ensuing climb along a series of lanes and sunken paths overgrown with brambles and even stinging nettles. The way comes out at a cluster of farms on a road close to a

2hr – ruined chapel (380m) in Romanesque style, and there is a curious prehistoric menhir in the adjacent field. The route turns west enclosed by old stone walls through farmland with views, eventually dropping through scrub to a road. Go left then first right for the little-used D181, and down to the crossroads of

Straightforward if not exceptionally exciting concluding stage of a wonderful long-distance experience. The destination Cargése is a good place to collapse, as it has a full range of creature comforts and the added attraction of beaches!

Curious menhir above Cargése - evidently broken up since the photo was taken!

50min – Cargèse (96m). Sun-soaked town with all supplies and services. Buses both directions. ① 04
95264131. Hôtel Punta e Mare ☎ 04 95264433, sleeps
20, has special rates for walkers except July–August, otherwise Hôtel Saint Jean ☎ 04 95264668 can cater for 32
year-round, but has no individual cooking facilities. Treat
yourself to a swim at splendid sandy Peru beach (Hotel
Ta Kladia ☎ 04 95264073, April–October), a 15min
stagger down the hill. Cargèse has a population of Greek
origin thanks to 16th-century refugees fleeing persecu-
tion under the Ottoman Empire.

Mare-Mare Nord: Cargèse to Moriani

Walking time	50hr 45min – 11 days
Distance	140.4km/87.1 miles
Difficulty	Grade 2
Maps	IGN 1:25,000 sheets 4151OT, 4150OT, 4250OT, 4351OT
Start	Cargèse
Finish	Moriani Plage

An exciting and highly recommended coast-to-coast
route that takes you right through the heart of Corsica.
Beginning on the stunning western side, it heads inland
via spectacular river gorges and high mountain passes
before reaching the island's ancient political and cultural centre, Corte. The concluding days see you mean-
dering through quiet hilltop villages before descending
to the lovely eastern seaboard looking to the Italian offshore islands. This is a challenging and strenuous but
immensely rewarding walk with several lengthy, tiring
stages, but there are also plenty of alternatives and
exit/entry points. Fit walkers could compress a couple
of days and complete the walk in 8–9 days if desired.
On the other hand it's fun allowing for days out to

At Col de Vergio

explore beauty spots – for example at Col de Vergio and Corte.

Suitable periods for this walk range from mid-April, when the vegetation on the coastal stretches is at its best, through midsummer, when the two 1500m passes are clear of snow and the high region provides welcome respite from the heat of the coast, right through to October/November, meteorological conditions and accommodation permitting.

Some memorable *gîtes d'étape* walkers' hostels provide lodging and nourishment en route, while a number of villages offer alternative accommodation in the shape of modest hotels. For the first two days, as far as Evisa, this route is in common with the popular Mare e Monti and makes use of the same signposting. It also means that accommodation is shared, so book ahead if possible to avoid disappointment. Moreover, remember that the otherwise excellent Refuge A Sega in Day 5 does not provide blankets, so you should theoretically carry a sleeping bag. However, having to lug one around with you for 11 days when it's only needed for a single night is not exactly attractive... you could always go to bed fully dressed!

55

If time is tight and choices need to be made to fit in with holiday dictates, the best section to do is probably the central four-day Evisa–Corte stretch, traversing the high mountain zones. Both start and finish have good bus services. In addition, numerous stages of this itinerary can be followed as day-walks.

Note: the Mare-Mare Nord is also referred to as the 'Traversale Nord: Moriani–Cargèse' on some signposting. Waymarking is orange paint stripes or metal markers on trees and prominent points, and is frequent and well maintained for the most part. Most people walk the route east to west, but the opposite direction as described here means you intersect other walkers and have the path to yourself more often. It's also fun and useful to swap information with people coming the other way. Note also that the official route on Day 10 has been modified and lengthened, so this up-to-date description differs slightly from most current maps at present.

Access: The township of Cargèse, where the route begins, is to be found on Corsica's mid-western coast, 51km north of the capital Ajaccio. The two are connected by year-round bus, which continues to Porto and Ota.

The village of Evisa, with year-round bus links to Ajaccio and a summer service to Corte and Porto, is a suitable point for joining – or leaving – the walk. After that, Col de Vergio is served by a summer bus (Porto–Corte), Albertacce and Calacuccia have year-long links to Corte (courtesy of the school bus), while well-connected Corte itself is on the Bastia–Ajaccio train line and many coaches pass through. On the final stages, feasible escapes can be made by bus from Castellare and Sermano (school period only) as well as Pied d'Alesani towards the coast, not to mention Tribbiolu and Castellana on the very last stretch. Moriani, the terminal of the Mare-Mare Nord, has daily year-round bus links with Bastia, and slightly less frequent runs south to Porto-Vecchio.

DAY 1: CARGÈSE TO E CASE

(total 5hr, 13km/8 miles, ascent/descent 910m/400m)

Cargèse (96m) – at the crossroads and monument over-looking the sea, take the D181 road northeast past a supermarket and signed for the Mare e Monte route. 10min up, as the coast to the south comes into view, fork left to where a marked path sets out through low scrub. There are lovely views to the retreating beaches along with the ubiquitous Genoese watchtower and far-off Capu Rossu. You climb steadily to a wide crest through rural properties and a series of gates before touching on a road and farms at

1hr 15min – ruined chapel (380m) of Romanesque design, together with a lone prehistoric menhir proudly re-erected by the locals in a field. Following signs for Lozzi, turn sharp left (north) down a shady path which reverts to an overgrown sunken lane thick with brambles and insidious nettles. This eventually joins a broad track leading to a stream ford (70m), where you go right (actually detouring the hamlet of **Lozzi**). Beneath old olive trees, following the Esigna stream and crossing back and forth in a heavily wooded valley topped by pink rock ridges, the track heads essentially east in imperceptible ascent for several kilometres. At around 190m, it crosses over to the left bank to loop up amidst dogs yapping to the huddle of shepherds' huts that go by the picturesque name of

1hr 45min – Bergeries de Santa Lucia (220m). From here a narrow path takes over for the steep scrambly haul northeast up through dry maquis. You follow a wire fence to gain a ridge (471m). A series of rock outcrops punctuate the lovely **Pianu Maggiore** crest bright with rock roses and broom. Views range across the rolling wooded hills and take in the hamlet of Revinda, as well as the coast. A little more ascent is needed (to 650m), then it levels out through an unusual wood of huge strawberry trees. A shady descent with masses of Corsican lilies leads to a welcome stream crossing where

Known as the town of the Greeks due to 16th-century refugees from the Ottoman Empire, laid-back Cargèse still boasts a handful of Greek-speaking inhabitants and its own Orthodox church. On the practical side, it has a full range of facilities for visitors, some lovely beaches and a choice of hotels and camping grounds. ⓘ 04 95264131. Hôtel Punta e Mare ☎ 04 95264433, sleeps 20, special rates for walkers except July–August, or Hôtel Saint Jean ☎ 04 95264668, sleeps 32 year-round, no cooking facilities.

The opening section of this great traverse consists of an alternation of steady climbs and descents. The culmination is a simple but memorable gîte d'étape.

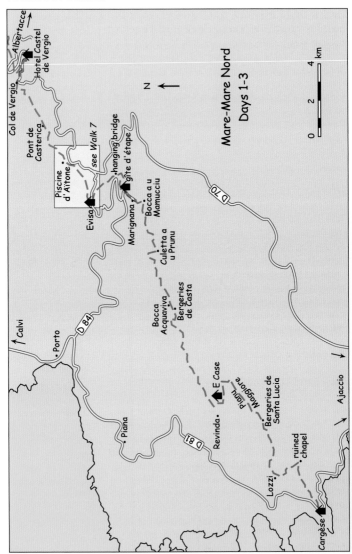

Mare-Mare Nord
Days 1-3

you'll want to cool off your feet. The concluding stretch northwest climbs slightly to the clearing and the isolated but remarkably scenic position of the *gîte d'étape*

2hr – E Case (605m). Overlooking the splendid Golfe de Chiuni, this converted stone farmhouse with rather basic facilities extends a lovely welcome to walkers. Meals are served *al fresco* and supplies are brought in by mule from the nearby roadhead at Revinda. ☎ 04 95264819 (guardian's house at Revinda) or mobile ☎ 06 82499565. Sleeps 22, open April–October.

DAY 2: E CASE TO MARIGNANA
(total 6hr, 17km/10.6 miles, ascent/descent 930m/825m)

Take the clear path through shoulder-high maquis, ignoring the turn-off left for Revinda a short way along. Proceeding northeast in shady wood you follow the minor thickly wooded valley of Rognia for a while, crossing countless streams before zigzagging decidedly uphill to a panoramic outcrop (960m) spread with lavender, juniper and asphodels. Marked by cairns the faint path soon reaches a series of circular stone enclosures (**Bergeries de Casta**) amidst scented broom. Past signs for a 'source', proceed above abandoned pasture to the distinct saddle of

3hr – Bocca Acquaviva (1102m). Set at the foot of modest Capu e Macenue, it offers vast views to distant inland mountains.

Maintaining the same direction, the route negotiates rougher loose stony terrain, threading its way through scratchy bushes in gradual diagonal descent. You will find an absolutely glorious range of splendid flowers in a wild beautiful area, miles from roads. Vestiges of the original mule track appear and lead into a dramatic red cleft valley.

A couple of stream crossings precede yet another climb – this time via a remarkable chestnut woods with

A very long stage, but particularly splendid and rewarding with extended wild stretches, glorious views and masses of wild flowers. Note that at the end, many walkers prefer to skip Marignana and press on for Evisa – a further 1hr 30min – where the accommodation has a better reputation. But be warned, it's a long haul.

ancient knobbly trees and welcome fresh green foliage. There are extraordinary monstrous exemplars. Past a ruined stone hut that once served as a *séchoir* for drying the chestnuts, the path winds up to a minor pass, **Culetta a u Prunu (970m)**, on open scenic ridge, affording views back to Bocca Acquavivia.

East-northeast the old mule track coasts through more crazily flowered slopes and across rock slabs, with views all the way down to Corsica's west coast. A chestnut copse is traversed to a rise, where a rough lane is encountered and you turn right in stumbling descent to

The old mule track negotiates stark gullies between E Case and Marignana

2hr 30min – Bocca a u Mamucciu (824m), cross and signed junction with a Mare-Mare Nord variant which breaks off southeast.

Turn left alongside the football field amidst pigs, foraging and lazing. Not far on are views to dramatic river gorges as the path quickly descends through the cobbled streets and modest stone dwellings of quiet

20min – Marignana (715m). Once you've reached the church, turn right along the road and past the cemetery for the

10min – *gîte d'étape* (also known as Ustaria di a Rota) ☎ 04 95262121, sleeps 40, always open. Groceries on sale. Year-round bus to Ajaccio.

DAY 3: MARIGNANA TO COL DE VERGIO
(total 5hr, 16.1km/10 miles, ascent/descent 880m/120m)

From the *gîte* take the path parallel to the road through chestnut woods for the gradual descent into a side valley to the evocative abandoned settlement of **U Tassu** (700m), which is worth exploring. You then drop steeply to a stream to cross it three times in quick succession, before traversing the Tavulella on a

30min – hanging bridge (635m).

The ensuing steep ascent through Mediterranean oak and maquis includes several lookout points over the tortuous road and gorge, then a gentler stretch follows an old wall in shady wood. After a stream crossing you climb via rough vehicle tracks to the road. Turn left for the nearby *gîte d'étape* on the lower reaches of

1hr – Evisa (850m). Well reputed *gîte* ☎ 04 95262188, sleeps 30, open April–October. A stroll away, the upper part of the village features grocery shops, a bakery and a handful of hotels, including U Pozzu, ☎ 04 95262289, sleeps 37, open April to mid-October. Year-round bus to Ajaccio; runs to Corte and Porto summer only.

Opposite the bakery (*boulangerie*) on the main road, you need the path signed for 'le Chemin des Châtaigniers' and the Piscine d'Aïtone which climbs via a concrete ramp to a Mare-Mare Nord signpost. Take the lane east past the pig sheds and information boards about chestnut harvesting and drying, once a principal activity in this region. A muddy stretch between old stone walls leads uphill to join the road briefly at a car park. Don't miss the detour to the great lookout point high over the Aïtone torrent. Straight afterwards is a broad lane left lined with foxgloves and lofty pines. This takes you past a picnic area with benches to a signed fork – keep left for the time being down high rock steps for the short detour to the

This marvellous day's walking takes in the magnificent Aïtone forest of towering Corsican pines, run through by a beautiful succession of cascades and attractive rock pools, not to mention photogenic suspension bridges. There are plenty of opportunities here for taking time out. The walk concludes at a medium altitude pass amidst exciting alpine scenery.

*At the Piscine
d'Aïtone*

1hr – Piscine d'Aïtone (910m) natural rock pools. A magnificent series of cascades and huge deep green pools shaded by the forest. Take care as the rocks can be slippery. Popular spot for family picnics.

Back up at the signed fork turn left (northeast) across a side stream and follow the pretty bank to a **suspension bridge** which leads to a steep ascent through stunning pine forest. This emerges on high to scramble over rock slabs colonised with bright broom shrubs. The ensuing gentle descent through fresh green beech trees approaches the Aïtone once again, past an unusable bridge hanging in threads.

Continue through the delightful forest of fir trees, holly and masses of tree heather to join a concrete-based forestry track (right) to nearby

1hr – Pont de Casterica (1170m) and more superb rock pools.

Just across the bridge, turn left for a clear, mostly level track through beech woods for around half an hour before an abrupt turn left. The steep slog follows a stony stream bed where encounters with roaming pigs are common. The wood eventually thins out, giving way to magnificent Corsican pines, accompanied by hellebore, asphodels and bracken. You finally reach the road pass popular with coach tours

1hr 15min – Col de Vergio (1478m) (or Col de Verghio). This watershed affords sweeping views down to the Calacuccia dam in the Niolo district. Kiosk with snacks and souvenirs, not to mention an impressive gigantic stone statue of Christ Roi atop a structure akin to an over-sized beehive. Summer buses.

Variant: If you're ploughing straight through from Col de Vergio and don't need the hotel, keep straight ahead on the marked Mare-Mare Nord trail, and subtract 30min from the timing.

In gentle descent southeast via the D84 bordered by slender silver birches, you are soon joined by the GR20 before gaining the area used for winter skiing around

15min – Hotel Castel de Vergio (1400m), ☎ 04 95480001, sleeps 80 in serviced rooms and basic dormitories. Frozen in a 1960s time warp, this cavernous, congenial – if a tad run-down – establishment caters for long-distance walkers with big appetites, and sells groceries and fresh fruit. The adjacent 'camping ground' in contrast is a scruffy gravel parking area. It's worth taking a day out here to do the Paglia Orba route – see Walk 8.

DAY 4: COL DE VERGIO TO ALBERTACCE
(total 4hr, 13km/8.1 miles, ascent/descent 160m/710m) ▶

From the hotel backtrack briefly up the road to where the red/white waymarked GR20 breaks off northwest through pretty thickets of silver birch and perfumed spurge. Several ups and downs later in the shade of numerous majestic Corsican pines you reach the intersection where

Today's route passes into the central uplands of the Niolo district through more forest with rivers and a picturesque Genoese bridge. Crowned by the island's highest peaks, the region was long renowned for harbouring bandits. It maintains its traditions of raising livestock and producing memorable ewe's milk cheeses. It also hosts a huge artificial lake.

At day's end, instead of overnighting at tiny Albertacce, those needful of a wider range of facilities (shops, restaurants, etc) will prefer continuing on to the next village, Calacuccia (see Day 5).

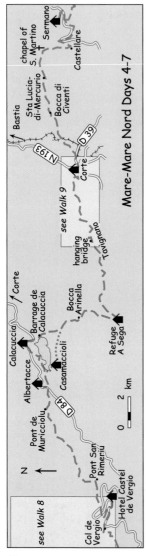

the Mare-Mare Nord turns sharp right (east). After a gradual descent in tall pine forest, it crosses the road twice and passes a military zone. The veritable maze of forestry tracks means you need to keep a constant eye out for orange paint stripes. About an hour downhill a pretty cascading side stream with lovely pools is encountered and, shortly, the mighty Golo river, having descended a fair way from where it rises at the foot of the Paglia Orba. A level track leads east to

1hr 20min – Pont San Rimeriu (1049m). The old bridge affords lovely views north-north-west to triangular Punta Licciola.

On the opposite bank climb straight ahead past a couple of huts (Bergerie de Tillerga) into mixed pine woods thick with lilies. The pleasant and clearly signed path moves northeast down the left side of the partially wooded valley, at times crossing open moorland populated by ferns, asphodels, broom and pungent herbs. Attractive wind-sculptured rock formations dot the way. Around 1hr 30min from the bridge is a marked fork (access to the GR20 and Cinque Frati Tour), with great mountain views: first and foremost due north is Corsica's highest peak, 2706m M. Cintu, spattered with snow in spring, while closer are the Cinque Frati to the north-north-west.

A flat stretch traverses shady chestnut woods then drops past a turn-off for an unrewarding 'Sentier Archéologique' to

2hr – Pont de Muricciolu (835m). A photogenic humpback bridge over the Viru and an old mill, not to mention a wonderful picnic and bathing spot. Exciting views west-north-west to Paglia Orba and Capu Tafunatu, along with the Cinque Frati once again.

Head east past a shrine and over an impressive gorge where the Viru flows into the Golo. Small-scale farms start to appear, and not far downhill is a road and prominent cross (**La Croix**) marking the southern entrance to the quiet village, a short distance left along the road.

To **detour** and continue through to Calacuccia, keep straight ahead.

40min – Albertacce (854m) has a modest museum of local archaeological finds as well as a well-reputed *gîte* ☎ 04 95480560, sleeps 20, open April–September. The Corte–Porto summer bus passes this way.

Pont de Muricciolu and the Cinque Frati

DAY 5: ALBERTACCE TO A SEGA

(total 5hr 15min, 12.4km/7.7 miles, ascent/descent 800m/460m)

Return to **La Croix** and the signed junction, picking up the trail to turn left (east) across scrubby overgrazed land to the lake's edge. Beneath chestnut trees a succession of dusty lanes shared with foraging pigs leads to a lakeside road, D218.

Here a slightly shorter variant via Casamaccioli breaks off south along the tarmac, avoiding Calacuccia. Casamaccioli (878m) *gîte* ☎04 95480347, sleeps 12, open April–October. The variant rejoins the main route during the climb to Bocca Arinella.

Climbing out of the Niolo, this exhilarating section incorporates the route's highest pass (1592m), which acts as an opening into the magnificent wild Tavignano valley. Try to make the lengthy ascent either early or late in the day, as it can be hot going in the noon sun.

Turn left for nearby sleepy **Sidossi** (800m), bar and restaurant, phone box outside the church. Soon after the bend in the lakeside road, take the signed old mule track left (northeast) that climbs gently to a cemetery, which is skirted left and the road reached. Turn right past the church for

1hr – Calacuccia (812m) and lovely old-style, rose-smothered Hôtel des Touristes ☎ 04 95480004, open May–October. It doubles as the *gîte* and offers special room rates for walkers (no cooking facilities). Breakfast is served, while dinner can be enjoyed at the nearby restaurants. Otherwise 10min west out of town is the modern hotel Acqua Viva ☎ 04 95480690, always open. Cafés and shops including chemist; year-round school bus to Corte and summer service to Porto. Handy base for climbing trips to the surrounding peaks, including the island's highest giant, M. Cintu. ① 04 95480522.

Climbing above the Calacuccia dam, view to Paglia Orba

Head south downhill towards the lake, turning right at the crossroads for the nearby dam

30min – Barrage de Calacuccia (794m). Constructed in 1968 to provide Bastia with a reliable water supply, its surface reflects the marvellous rugged mountains that rise beyond the broad Niolo valley.

At the far end of the wall a marked path heads essentially south, confused at times with sheep tracks. Ascending steadily amidst scrubby vegetation, it cuts the wide curves of a dirt track passing herder's modest abodes. As you climb there are great views back northwest over the lake to Cinque Frati, Paglia Orba and neighbours. Further up, the easy zigzags of an ancient mule track are followed, taking the sting out of what would otherwise be a steep climb. Passing across windswept land populated by grazing herds of cows and sheep, you finally reach the broad open crest and fence marking

2hr 30min – Bocca Arinella (1592m). Amazing panorama of mountains and valleys any way you look! A magnificent pair of red kites can often be seen surveying the ridge for audacious rodents.

A marked track leads off southeast to cross a laneand pass the cluster of huts that constitute the **Bergerie de Boniacce** (1500m). The descent south now begins in earnest towards the very promising wild wooded valley at your feet. Incredible concentrations of the showy white Corsican lily are traversed on the edge of the conifer woods, which gradually gather force and provide real shade as you zigzag down approaching the river. A final stretch to the right takes you through to

1hr 15min – Refuge A Sega (1190m) ☎ 04 95460790 (guardian's house at Corte – his wife takes the bookings and passes them on via radio) or mobile ☎ 06 10717726 (frequently no reception). Sleeps 36, open May–October. No blankets provided. Unassuming but surprising spacious modern construction stunningly placed on the banks of the Tavignano river. Opened in 2002, it extends a warm welcome to walkers and serves delicious home-

Stunning setting of Refuge A Sega

This entire day is spent in the magnificent Tavignano river valley cloaked with a memorable forest of towering, perfectly straight Corsican pines, many of which unfortunately bear the telltale signs of the terrible fires that swept through in the summer of 2000. The valley narrows to a deep gorge in the middle section.

made dishes. Supplies are brought in on horseback from the roadhead at the *bergerie* passed above.

DAY 6: A SEGA TO CORTE

(total 4hr 15min, 12km/7.4 miles, ascent/descent 100m/770m)

A stone's throw away, a new timber bridge affords a wonderful view of the brilliant green waters of the Tavignano cascading through inviting if chilly rock pools. The pale granite banks are coloured delicate hues under the effect of rainbow lichens and splashes of broom. On the opposite bank you pass the decrepit hut and former refuge … consider yourself lucky you didn't have to spend the night there!

Cruising easily northeast initially, the Mare-Mare Nord follows the course of the river closely at first then lets it drop dramatically through a series of steep-sided ravines. As the mountainside becomes steeper, the path cuts a safe if narrow passage between sadly charred pine trees, dizzily high above the crashing river. It reveals itself to be a former mule track, an incredible feat of engineering with surprisingly long stretches still intact thanks to stone reinforcing and paving. It's a matter of continual ups and downs, the route weaving its way between crazy rock points with giddy views. Several side streams are crossed, and only at the last moment does the track make up its mind to actually descend in earnest to the level of the watercourse and the long-awaited

2hr – bridge (760m), Lovely place to cool off in rock pools. The atmosphere on the opposite bank of the Tavignano is dramatically different as the pine forest disappears abruptly. This is the realm of drier maquis shrubs such as tree heather, Mediterranean oak and the colourful scented blooms of broom and lavender.

Wider and regularly paved, the path proceeds essentially east, the lower vegetation affording plenty of views of totem-pole-like rock needles, as well as the plunging river bed below. The township of Corte is soon glimpsed, and another side stream and pool encountered. A surprisingly dense mass of white rock rose shrubs is traversed, followed by maritime pines with red fissured bark. A tabernacle precedes abandoned terracing before the final ups and downs as you pass a well-kept shrine and reach the road on the outskirts of Corte. A further 15min are needed for the township and hotels (straight ahead down Rue St-Joseph); however for the *gîte* (same timing) take Chemin de Baliri, the first road to the right in descent, then turn right again across the now placid Tavignano. After a parking area, a lane winds up to the peaceful shady spot of U Tavignanu ☎ 04 95461685, sleeps 20, open year-round. Also camping ground. Laid-back family-run establishment with excellent meals. No self-catering. Advance booking recommended.

2hr 15min – Corte (420m) ⓘ 04 95462670. Trains to Ajaccio, Bastia and Calvi, as well as coaches in virtually all directions. All supplies and services. Hotel La Poste ☎ 04 95460137. Corte is a great place for taking time out – visit the charming historic town with its steep cobbled streets, tottering houses, and fountains and belvedere citadel; listen to traditional men's chanting-singing; visit the neighbouring Restonica valley (Walk 10); and last but not least stock up on food, as no further shops are encountered on the final four days of the Mare-Mare Nord until Moriani Plage, at the very end.

DAY 7: CORTE TO SERMANO

(total 5hr 30min, 16.9km/10.5 miles, ascent/descent 950m/620m) ◀

The excitement of Corte and its magnificent mountain valleys behind you, this day traverses the quiet rural district of Boziu and touches on a number of scenically placed villages with the odd frescoed medieval chapel. While the landscapes tend towards arid and bare, in compensation they swarm with roaming pigs, grazing sheep, cattle and even horses, and birds of prey are a common sight. A number of abrupt climbs and subsequent drops make the walk somewhat tiring.

From the point where the Mare-Mare Nord leaves the Tavignano at the rear of the citadel of Corte, take Rue St-Joseph in descent to a crossroads then go left and a quick right down to cross Boulevard Paoli (facing Hotel du Nord). Turn left past a souvenir shop to drop via Avenue Jean Nicoli, past a car park and university premises, to the river and a major intersection (398m), close to the railway station. Now, straight ahead, you need the D39, a quiet country road signed for Sermano.

A mere 5min along you are pointed off left (northeast) for a lane, and soon find yourself in green fields and gently rolling hills populated by herds of sheep grazing amidst rock rose shrubs. A stream (the Bistugliu) is soon crossed, as is the single-track **railway line** soon afterwards. There are lovely views back over Corte to snow-specked mountains, though these improve notably during the climb ahead. Signed for Santa Lucia, the route leads in steady ascent via cool sunken lanes crammed with ferns to a dry, over-grazed hillside culminating at

1hr 40min – Bocca di Civenti (785m). Ample saddle, where panoramas include prominent M. Rotondo southwest over the Restonica valley with its overlapping waves of ridges.

The clear path proceeds east cutting a dry hillside thick with marvellous aromatic maquis herbs before negotiating steep cobbled alleys leading to the scenic square of

50min – Sta Lucia-di-Mercurio (820m). Pretty, well-kept village with sweeping views and drinking water.

Moving off in the company of honeysuckle and dog roses east to drop via a succession of hamlets to a road then light wood cover, the route follows a modest valley with a trickling stream. Chestnut trees make their appearance, then shady Mediterranean oak takes over. You climb to cross a road and soon emerge on a high ridge at

1hr – Chapel of San Martino (904m). The views here even take in far-off M. Cintu, recognisable west-northwest.

A series of tight zigzags drop south down the hillside enlivened by striking low bushes of woolly yellow button flowers, noisy jays and wood pigeons. You coast through scented elderberry and poppies into quiet

40min – Castellare (610m). Drinking fountain outside the church. School-days bus link with Corte.

Descend past loaded cherry trees, the landmark phone box and left for a ramp lined with curious Indian bead trees to the D241. A short stretch north and you break off right just after the cemetery to embark on a shady sunken way northeast to a **stream crossing** (565m).

As usual, any descent is followed by a stiff climb, and the D41 is cut on several occasions. As the wood comes to an end, barren hillside takes over and M. d'Oro with its trademark knobbly point is clearly recognisable southwest, while much closer at hand is Col de Bozio, east. After a **path junction** (Mare-Mare variant for Poggio Venaco and looping back to Corte) you

Old houses in Sermano, backed by Monte d'Oro

bear left (northeast) on a level for the last leg, the village now visible not too far ahead. A ramp leads past the cemetery and the 12th-century frescoed **Chapelle San Niculau** (hopefully open) and up into the pretty village of

1hr 10min – Sermano (750m). Bus on school days to/ from Corte. At the main road turn right for the *gîte*. A final 1km along a panoramic road to a turn-off left at the helicopter landing pad, and it's not far to

10min – U San Fiurenzu, Chez Simon ☎ 04 95486808, sleeps 24, open April–October, no kitchen facilities. Recently refurbished comfortable place with a lovely terrace for drying your laundry or enjoying a well-earned beer in contemplation of all those hills you've trudged across.

DAY 8: SERMANO TO PIANELLU

(total 4hr 45min, 12.2km/7.6 miles, ascent/descent 560m/530m)

Return to **Sermano** (750m) and take the marked route past the post office and down the cobbled laneways to a cross and huddle of restored stone houses where you are pointed left. A pleasant old way descends gradually amidst pretty dog roses into lovely wooded Valle Rosso and across side streams to a **derelict mill** (615m). An almost ghostly corridor with blackened tree trunks winds around east to climb easily southwards to the road at

1hr 30min – Alando (710m). Drinking fountain, phone box. There is a recommended signposted 10min-return detour to the adjacent knoll of Tozza, where you climb to a brilliant belvedere and enamelled *table d'orientation* showing all the landmarks for 360°. Views range from Alcudine, south-southwest, through M. d'Oro, west-southwest, twin peaks M. Cardu and Punta Lattiniccia, west, and M. Cintu to the west-northwest.

Turn left along the road via a sizeable monument for a 14th-century patriot and liberator to a rambling **old convent** (café and drinking water). Keep right on the D339 past Chez Laurent's bar, where you're pointed downhill (southeast) across another watercourse. At a smelly pig sty turn left onto a lane uphill beneath chestnut trees and through the hamlet of **Alzi** (780m). The ensuing rise affords lovely views over neighbouring hamlets resting on wooded flanks, their slate roofs red and grey.

The road is rejoined briefly as far as picturesque **Mazzola** (900m), then a clear path heads up northeast through wood, cutting the road and going past a spring to join a narrow road left for spectacularly located hilltop **Castelluccio** (975m). It comprises a handful of traditional houses currently undergoing renovation and a cool, life-saving well with built-in benches shaded by a walnut tree. Views range all the way back over the previous day's route.

A further tiring but rewarding day up and down hill and dale, dropping in on well-placed picturesque hamlets, and traversing a long wild ridge that culminates in a particularly friendly village and another well-reputed *gîte*. Take care at signposted turn-offs in this region, as the web of local paths can be confusing. The Mare-Mare Nord is always waymarked in orange.

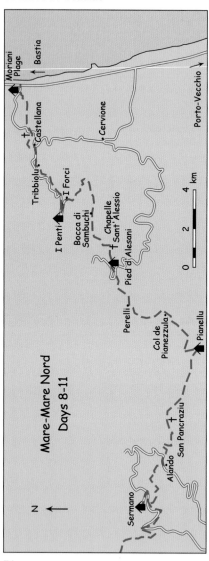

Mare-Mare Nord
Days 8–11

Now it's not far in steady ascent through chestnut woods thick with ferns to an outcrop known as

1hr 30min – San Pancraziu (1020m). Unpretentious chapel with a marvellous outlook. This point marks the trail's farewell to the mountainous interior once and for all, as you begin to breathe in the scent of the sea and get promising glimpses. The level route east leads to delightful fresh green beech woods as you follow a crest high above pasture land. Later on the terrain opens out to maquis cover of tree heather and asphodels, inhabited by cuckoos and chaotic wood pigeons, and with a good chance of birds of prey.

You dip across a dirt track and a watercourse then climb briefly to a ridge and lane, where you now have a wonderful view all the way down to the coastal plain and the glittering sea, along with villages strung out below. A clear path across slabs sparkling with mica leads to the first apparently deserted settlement of **Poggio**, where waymarking all but disappears. Follow your nose down the linking lanes heading for the prominent church of

1hr 45min – Pianellu (803m), opposite the gleaming council-owned *gîte*, ☎ 04 95396135 (the guardian's home at Ghisonaccia) or mobile ☎ 06 81471895, sleeps 18, open April–October. The cavernous refurbished building has spacious dormitories and modern bathrooms, while the ground floor doubles as the local community centre.

DAY 9: PIANELLU TO PIED D'ALESANI
(total 4hr, 8.9km/5.5 miles, ascent/descent 620m/743m)

Leave the *gîte* along the road past the council offices and livestock enclosures to the helicopter landing pad and intersection where you turn left (north) on the D16. A kilometre or so in gentle descent lined with heady broom will see you at a stone bridge, **Pont sur la Bravona** (740m). Not far on a signed path breaks off left for a steady climb east through a wood of chestnut and ferns and masses of wild mint underfoot. The vegetation thins considerably as you approach a sloping crest with a sweep of vistas taking in the sea, Pianellu and even as far back as the snow-capped peaks over Corte.

Shadeless now, the ascent continues northeast taking you through clumps of Corsican hellebore and tree heather, the habitat of scampering rabbits. A level stretch of path across moorland leads to a grassy saddle, namely

This region is known as the Castagniccia for its bountiful chestnuts and the inhabitants' traditional reliance on the tree for their livelihood. Long wild stretches across uplands alternate with farming villages. Enticing views to the coast have become a constant companion.

1hr 30min – Col de Pianezzula (1083m), one of a series of minor cols of similar altitude.

Not long afterwards the path veers markedly north and starts its gradual descent through woods of hawthorn, chestnut and oak. A good way down you cross a road for a lane through to the hamlet of

1hr 20min – Perelli (750m), drinking fountain, white stuccoed church that doubles as home to chattering swifts.

Past the École (school) is the start of a knee-jarring drop to the intersection at **Casella** (2km detour right for the historic Couvent d'Alesani). Close to the chapel you'll need to hunt around for the faintly marked rough path that crashes its way through chaotic woodland, inhabited by pungent goats and woodpeckers, to finally emerge on a lower road. Turn left here (signed for Pied d'Alesani) over a grey **stone bridge** (450m) to where a path soon branches up left. Chestnuts and squawking crows keep you company through dense undergrowth for the stiff path to a minor road, where signs point you right for the *gîte d'étape* at

1hr 10min – Pied d'Alesani (680m). Brand new council-run hostel, ☎ 04 95359474 or mobile 06 32953930, sleeps 22, open March/April to early October. Year-round bus to the coast and Bastia.

DAY 10: PIED D'ALESANI TO I PENTI
(total 4hr 15min, 9.8km/6.1 miles, ascent/descent 460m/525m)

Return to where you turned off for the *gîte* and go uphill via ramps, avoiding the bulk of the village. At signboards and a fountain go sharp right (due east) for a steep climb through more chestnuts, including exceptional exemplars. These give way to scented maquis which takes you through to

1hr 15min – Chapelle Sant'Alessio (960m). Marvellous lookout point to the Tyrrhenian and the Italian island of Elba. A section northeast following the contour line boasts low maquis studded with abundant wild flowers and accompanied by cooling sea breezes. Then comes an especially scenic ridge terminating at bizarrely named Col Frate Mortu ('dead monk pass'!) not long before the ample grassy saddle

1hr – Bocca di Sambuchi (911m). This is where the new routing begins, a worthwhile panoramic extension. (The original route headed straight down through

A long, enjoyably solitary traverse of rolling hills and a string of superb ridges is undertaken before finally embarking on the drop to a *gîte* which is also a top-rate restaurant.
Note: the final section of this day's load has been officially re-routed and lengthened a fair bit. Most maps still show the old routing, so don't be perplexed by discrepancies.

the thick wood, but erosion and landslips have made the new path necessary.)

Keep right (due east) as per signs for Castellu on a narrow but clear path that climbs to the 1000m mark. It passes to the left of M. Castellu, with great views over wild wooded valleys and to the glittering sea. On a flat, open crest (900m) you find yourself facing the modest rise of M. Negrine, absolutely smothered in broom. Signposting (bearing over-optimistic timing) reappears, and you're pointed sharp left (northwest) down amidst blooming hawthorn. Waymarking is red and orange paint stripes now. You swing down into a side valley and zigzag down beneath chestnuts which give way to a jungle of creepers and vines. Following a stream, two concrete bridges need crossing, then it's up into the peaceful hamlet of

1hr 45min – I Forci (605m). A marked corner-cutting route breaks off right (northeast) here, detouring I Penti, a saving of 30min.

At the opposite end of the old terrace-style dwellings a shady road takes you west-northwest to

15min – I Penti (615m) and the *gîte d'étape* Luna Piena ☎ 04 95385948, sleeps 20, open April–October. This final establishment on the Mare-Mare Nord boasts a garden for guests and a lovely shady setting on an 'island' between streams and photogenic stone bridges. Though the reception verges on gruff, lots of positive energy is dedicated to the high quality catering. The village of I Penti, a tranquil, minuscule affair, is a mere stone's throw away and worth exploring.

DAY 11: I PENTI TO MORIANI PLAGE
(total 2hr 45min, 9.1km/5.6 miles, ascent/descent 40m/655m)

Take the D34 downhill, ignoring the fork to I Penti proper. Just around the bend take the path off right (yellow/orange,

The waymarking leaves a lot to be desired on this concluding section to sea level, so allow plenty of extra time.

marked for the nearby ferruginous spring Acqu-Acitosa). It runs parallel to the road and passes scattered tombs before veering right and down to cross the stream, draped with all manner of chaotic greenery. Not far along a larger watercourse is traversed and you bear left (northeast). A lengthy level stretch along the riverbank ensues, via chestnut woods and lush green paddocks featuring tassel hyacinths, eventually fording the unpronounceable Buccatoghju.

It's not far up to a drinking fountain on the edge of scenically located

1hr – Tribbiolu (515m). Towering slender stone dwellings and lovely views to the sea with the Italian island of Elba and its satellites. School bus to Moriani. An atmospheric old paved track winds down, thick with wild mint and bracken. Below a chapel (belonging to Repiola, which is bypassed) an asphalt road alternates with a path for the remaining distance into

30min – Castellana (269m), set on a brilliant terrace overlooking the glittering Tyrrhenian. School bus to Moriani. Turn left behind the chapel and continue through the village to the Mairie, then a path resumes in chestnut woods. A water treatment plant, where the first cork oaks appear, is followed by a lane through to the renowned Baroque **church of San Nicolao**. Take the lane opposite, forking left at the nearby intersection to swing back close to the tarmac. Go right at the next branch past houses to a better-marked series of lanes and roads leading into a residential zone. At the T-junction with a restaurant (I Lampioni) turn right for the main coast road, N198, and

1hr 15min – Moriani Plage ① 04 95384173. Not the island's most exciting beach, but it does offer shops, ice cream, accommodation and daily buses to Bastia and Porto-Vecchio. Auberge de Jeunesse L'Avillanella (Youth Hostel) ☎ 04 95385010, 2km south of town, with beach access. Open May–October.

Mare-Mare Sud:
Porto-Vecchio to Propriano

Walking time	26hr 35min – 5 days
Distance	77km/48.1 miles
Difficulty	Grade 2
Maps	IGN 1:25,000 sheets 4254ET, 4254OT, 4253OT
Start	Porto-Vecchio
Finish	Propriano

'I have seen the southern part of the Island pretty thoroughly. Its inner scenery is magnificent – a sort of Alpine character with more southern vegetation impresses you, & the vast pine forests unlike those of gloomy dark monotonous firs of the north, are green and varied Pinus Maritima. Every corner of the place not filled up by great Ilex trees and pines and granite rocks is stuffed with cistus and arbutus, Laurustinus, lent & heath: and the remaining space if any is all cyclamen & violets, anemones & asphodels – let alone nightingales and blackbirds.'

Edward Lear on his visit in the 1860s

A glorious coast-to-coast traverse of a great slice of southern Corsica from the Golfe de Porto-Vecchio and its superb white sand beaches in the east over to Propriano and the Golfe de Valinco in the west. This was an ancient area for human settlements dating back to prehistory, and is also known as the 'Terre des Seigneurs', a reference to its prominence in feudal times. Nowadays it is renowned for its laid-back atmosphere and as one of the greenest regions on the island, with high-altitude plateaux for livestock grazing.

The route entails long expanses of shady evergreen oak and pine forests intervalled by the hospitable villages of the Alta Rocca region with their superb high mountain scenery, as well as frequent delightful river crossings, welcome in the heat of the day for a dip and perfect for restful picnic lunches. No particular difficulty is involved though the usual rule applies of being fit enough to deal with constant climbs and drops which can be tiring. It is the most straightforward of the long-distance routes described, suitable for starters, with an average day's walking load of 5 hours. In warm weather start out early, use sun protection and take plenty of drinking water. The odd grocery store is encountered in the villages for supplies, otherwise the *gîtes d'étape* will do packed lunches on request. It's a popular walk and the well-run *gîtes* are best booked ahead in peak season.

April–June then September–October are the best periods for the Mare-Mare Sud as the summer can get suffocatingly hot at the medium altitudes. It is feasible all year round though some snow cover can be expected on the higher sections midwinter. Several *gîtes d'étape* are permanent establishments ie open year-round, however they may close up without notice when work drops off. As per all the long-distance routes, way-marking is a single orange paint stripe, faded at times, but fairly constant.

A number of intriguing detours are feasible and are referred to in the text: the Piscia di Gallo waterfall, Zonza whence the magnificent Col de Bavella, not to mention the prehistoric site of Cucuruzzu.

Note: the initial stage entails a 7km stretch of sur-faced if quiet road, which can be avoided by taking the bus from Porto-Vecchio up the hill to L'Ospedale. The concluding section of the walk (after Burgo) likewise embodies a rather uninteresting 7km of road, not an especially satisfying way to conclude such a rewarding walk. One way out is to take the bus from Ste Lucie de Tallano straight to Propriano, or bail out at Fozzano.

Porto-Vecchio is a lovely place to start the walk. Constructed by the Genoese in the 16th century as a rampart against pirate attacks, the town and its citadel stand high on a pink porphyry base overlooking a broad bay edged with productive salt pans. An interesting if rather touristy town, with access to some excellent beaches, it has plenty of hotels, camping grounds, super-markets, medical services and buses. ⓘ 04 95700958. Hotel Panorama ☎ 04 95700796.

Access: Porto-Vecchio lies on the far south-eastern coast of Corsica, and is served by several coach lines (links with Bastia, Bonifacio and Ajaccio) not to mention inter-national ferries in summer. The destination, Propriano, on the south-western coast, has similar plentiful trans-port links.

To help with entering or leaving the walk at interme-diate villages, the summer months mean a weekday Ajaccio to Porto-Vecchio bus via L'Ospedale, Zonza and Serra di Scopameno, as well as a Propriano to Porto-Vecchio run, handy for returning to the start point.

DAY 1: PORTO-VECCHIO TO CARTALAVONU
(total 5hr 10min, 15.1km/9.4 miles, ascent 1000m)

Porto-Vecchio (50m) – from the town centre and Place de la République take the road northwest down past the Hôtel de Ville. At the foot of the hill is a camping ground where you bear right (north) towards a four-road inter-section Quatre Chemins with a prominent hypermarket. Turn left (northwest) on the D368 for L'Ospedale, and not far along, before the roundabout, it's left again along Rue des Turriccioli (Park signpost). Through a wood of cork trees is a roundabout – 2nd left. A good way on past rural properties, fork right (signs for Nota) and through thinning maquis the cluster of buildings at L'Ospedale on the ridge ahead comes into view. A further signed fork leads left across a torrent followed by a grazing plain dotted with farms. A gradual climb past a couple of houses and you're at

1hr 45min – Alzu di Gallina (140m) which consists of a single dwelling. Official signposting for the Mare-Mare Sud can be found on the right-hand side of the road. A dry sandy path strikes out through luxuriant aromatic maquis starring lavender and native rock roses. You join

This introductory sec-tion is distinguished by a steady climb through markedly dif-fering vegetation bands, namely aro-matic coastal Mediterranean plants to the wonders of a superb pine forest on a medium altitude plateau.

81

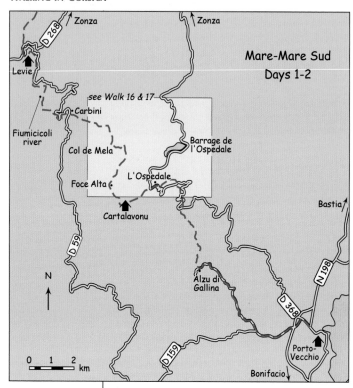

Mare-Mare Sud
Days 1–2

a broad track briefly and climb to a ridge with sweeping views of Porto-Vecchio and its gulf. Maritime pines gradually gain the upper hand over the shrubs and a dense wood ensues with welcome shade. The path cuts across the asphalt road a total of five times, before coasting left through a zone colonised by ferns and into

2hr 45min – L'Ospedale (880m) Bar-restaurant, limited food supplies, summer bus. Modest stone houses sit amongst a cascade of granite boulders, and there are magnificent views of the coast and mountainous Sardinia.

Following the road you quickly find yourself in the Fôret de l'Ospedale, a cool dense canopy of towering pines and varied undergrowth of foxgloves, wild strawberries and hellebore. Not far up the road is the turn-off left for Cartalavonu. ▶

A restful stretch leads southwest through pretty wood thick with orchids, to emerge on the lightly wooded plateau housing the *gîte d'étape*-farm at

40min – Cartalavonu (1020m). Le Refuge ☎ 04 95700039, sleeps 44, open April to early October. Rambling establishment run by a cantankerous family, but they do a good dinner.

DAY 2: CARTALAVONU TO LEVIE
(total 4hr 40min, 12.9km/8.1 miles, ascent/descent 540m/950m)

Take the lane northwest through light wood amongst rock roses, lavender and the ubiquitous pungent everlasting plant. Don't be tempted to follow the red paint marks but stick to the orange stripes. A track is joined briefly leading to a climb via a panoramic stone-studded hill flank with wonderful clumps of bright broom as well as views across to Sardinia. The way bears northwest and the Barrage de l'Ospedale becomes visible prior to the ample panoramic saddle of

30min – Foce Alta or Bocca Alta (1171m).

At this point you can break off for the **variant** via the breathtaking 1314m Punta di a Vacca Morta (see Walk 16), and rejoin the main route at Col de Mela. An extra 200m and 30min are entailed and a decent sense of orientation and some scrambling required.

A delightful **detour** is feasible here: stick to the road (D368) north for the interesting Ospedale lake-cum-dam 3km on, then it's a further 2km for the Piscia di Gallo waterfall (1hr from the Cartalavonu turn-off – see Walk 17). Hitchhiking is possible, as there is plenty of tourist traffic.

Rolling wooded hills with some great views characterise this second day, and there are several steep sections to test your walking legs. A couple of villages with curious historical links are encountered.

Continuing north-northeast the clear path follows the undulating mountainside around to the pass marked by a hut and minor roadhead

30min – Col de Mela (1068m) aka Bocca a Mela. The descent towards the village of Carbini commences gently amidst scattered granite boulders and pine forest to traverse a damp zone pitted with hoof marks and scratchings left by wild pigs. It starts dropping in earnest rather unexpectedly with innumerable winds, zigzags and stone steps. The Bavella rock needles are clearly visible to the north and hamlets and farms begin to appear below as the vegetation thins a little, and Mediterranean species such as holm oak, strawberry tree take over from the higher pines. Shady and cool best describe it. Chestnut trees precede a dirt track which is crossed for an old path flanked by simple stone walls. A little care is needed for the odd detour to traverse boulder-choked streams. A lane leads past isolated houses and you finally emerge at rather characterless

Church at Carbini

1hr 30min – Carbini (560m). Snack bar, public phone. The village boasts a photogenic Romanesque church in Pisan style dating back to the 12th century with a distinct bell-tower. The site is sadly renowned for the massacre of the intriguing 'heretic' Giovannali sect in

the 1300s. Sincerely preaching and practising poverty, they were seen as a serious challenge to the church hierarchy, which led to their ultimate excommunication and untimely violent end. However in a final 'mystic' touch, doves were said to have emerged from the funeral pyres and flown off towards the mountains.

Waymarking resumes opposite the church and you head for the far end of the cemetery before dropping left to cut the D59 road twice and plunging into dense wood of evergreen oak. An old sunken path lined by mossy banks and a stone wall leads west in decisive descent to ford the **Fiumicicoli river** (220m). In normal conditions it's a simple matter of balancing on prominent stones.

The clear way north now climbs steeply and relentlessly through closely growing oaks. It passes an abandoned olive grove complete with an old press (Uvezza) and you have to watch out for your legs on this stretch as tall bracken conceals insidious nettles. The path runs parallel to the quiet road, and a couple of easy stream crossings precede a final short climb towards the outlying houses of Levie hung with climbing roses. A surfaced road leads you towards the church, but before reaching it you are pointed left past the cemetery to the *gîte*.

2hr 10min – Levie (610m). Immaculately kept *gîte* ☎ 04 95784641, sleeps 25, open April to October. ⓘ 04-95784195 (summer only), bus, restaurants and food shops. The local archaeological museum gives a good introduction to Corsican prehistory through finds from the nearby sites of Cucuruzzu and Capula, and also boasts the 6570 BC skeleton dubbed the Dame de Bonifacio, the oldest vestige of a human on the island.

DAY 3: LEVIE TO SERRA DI SCOPAMENA
(total 6hr, 18km/11.2 miles, ascent/descent 750m/510m)

Signposting starts at the church pointing the route north through the peaceful village of Levie. After a concrete ramp then a fountain and some asphalt, a delightful

A string of hospitable villages alternates with wild mountain-sides, watercourses and rockscapes.

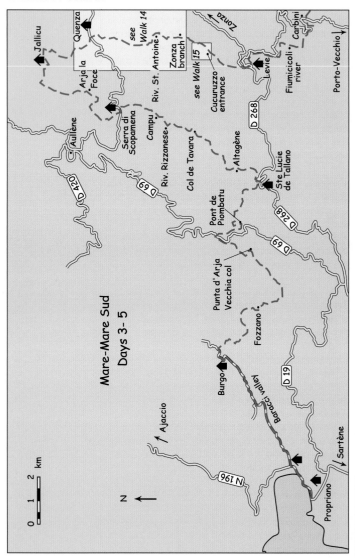

Mare-Mare Sud
Days 3- 5

paved path breaks off to the left. Continuing north it emerges on a grassy plain and turns right as a narrow surfaced road signed for the 'Sites Archeologiques' in sight of the Bavella needles. Soon after the car park is the

40min – entrance for Cucuruzzu (760m), a warmly recommended detour to a fascinating Bronze Age settlement and archaeological site (see Walk 15). Rucksacks can be left at the ticket booth as it entails a 1-2hr loop and you'll need to return in any case to bring back the walkman included in the self-guided visit.

The broad cool lane continues in a northerly direction past a pretty Romanesque chapel (St Laurent) close to the Capula settlement, visitable as above. Quieter now

Stream near
Rivière St Antoine

and shaded by a range of Mediterranean oaks, it descends very gradually between moss-ridden stone walling to

30min – branch for Zonza (730m) see Walk 14 for the recommended detour to a scenic village at the foot of the spectacular Col de Bavella area.

Proceed downhill more decidedly to ford a modest stream in an area bright with showy orange lilies, then the new bridge over the **Rivière St Antoine** (568m). A wire fence is followed northwest up a dry hillside to an enclosure, ostensibly for breeding re-introduced deer. Here a lane lined with heady broom goes right. Keep right at the ensuing fork (left is a rough lane to Sorbollana, useful as a short cut to Serra di Scopamena). A kilometre or so north means scrubby wood and undulating pastureland, keeping left at a fork in the track, before a brief drop in sight of Quenza. The final stretch of the climb is via a narrow path through a surprising thicket of honeysuckle, wild mint and orchids alongside a stream. In the company of rather enthusiastic dogs, a road takes over to lead you past old water troughs and up to a park with ancient chestnut trees opposite the 11th century church at

1hr 45min – Quenza (820m). Hotel (Sole e Monti ☎ 04 95786253, open April to October), groceries, bus, camping ground and congenial *gîte d'étape* 1km east of the village, Odyssée ☎ 04 95786405, sleeps 36, open end March to end October, no cooking facilities.

A signpost opposite the church points you northwest along the road, which you leave after 200 metres for a bridge over a stream. A series of old paths and lanes then climb steadily and cross the road near Buri. Continuing through chestnut and holly bushes, you eventually emerge on the dry hillsides of the vast Coscionu plateau. Superb for lone ski tourers in winter, it is better known as a key pastoral plain watered by a surprising number of streams, and punctuated by dozens of dry stone shepherds' huts. Low cairns show the way through bushes of wild roses, cistus and the aromas of thyme and everlasting. An abrupt turn left onto a lane leads to the nearby road and sparse dwellings of

1hr 15min – Jallicu aka Ghjallicu (1110m) and the *gîte d'étape* alias horse riding establishment ☎ 04 95786321, sleeps 18, open year-round, no cooking facilities. An overnight stay here really means getting away from it all.

The route sticks to the narrow road until signposting points you off right plunging back into the maquis. Past

an old mill once used for crushing chestnuts is a delightful cascading stream (978m), the perfect spot for a cool
rest. On the other side are the characteristic stone shepherds' huts of Lavu Donacu (45min) in rather bare wild
surrounds dominated by the rugged rock ridges of Punta
Illarata to the northwest. You bear southwest to a nondescript col spelt as Arghja Petrosa or similar (1014m) and
a variant west for Aullène. Flanking ploughed fields you
go due south across the Pianu Sottanu plain, a level
expanse of 'heathland' with an unusual number of
scratchy spiky shrubs that leave their mark, and scented
pinks. After a saddle (**Arja la Foce**, 1040m) is some welcome shade. Huge orange arrows guide you through a
maze of tracks to a signed junction (Bocca di Paradisu,
969m). Keep straight ahead down on the jeep track south
pass the camping ground. On reaching the main road at
an elaborate votive shrine, turn left for

1hr 50min – Serra di Scopamena (850m) and the hospitable, spotless and panoramically placed *gîte d'étape*
☎ 04 95786490, sleeps 26, open April to October.
Grocery shop downstairs, bus service. A matter of minutes around the corner the charming village nestles in
the elbow of the valley, its cosy houses adorned with
climbing roses and geraniums.

DAY 4: SERRA DI SCOPAMENA TO STE LUCIE DE TALLANO
(total 4hr, 9.7km/6.1 miles, ascent/descent 400m/800m)

Another cooling river and straightforward woodland traverse leads to a memorable village.

On the western edge of the village past the post office,
take the signed path opposite attractive Café di
l'Universu dropping between the houses, keeping right
at the first turn-off. A detour is feasible left for Serra's
restored mill. The old paved path follows the line of the
cleft valley and a trickling stream, passing a fork for
Sorbollano. Majestic oaks and chestnuts provide most of
the shade, along with abandoned fruit trees. After the
ruined hamlet of Mamma, you join the D20 for a brief
stretch downhill to Campu (400m) where the path takes

Rivière Rizzanese

up again. A minor watercourse is crossed and its shady bank followed to a long wooden bridge over the

1hr 20min – Rivière Rizzanese (380m). A wonderful place for a refreshing dip or just a laze on the smooth rocks on the bank. However, keep your wits about you as the river appears in numerous tales of mesmerising fairies enchanting local shepherds...

Of course after the easy descent comes the inevitable ascent – a long one too! A clear path heading decidedly south through oak woods, climbs stiffly at times. An open area of bracken is finally reached, and you can see back to Serra di Scopamena on its wooded hillside perch in the foreground of a marvellous natural amphitheatre, and even the Bavella Aiguilles are visible. Not far along is the high point, **Col de Tavara** (720m).

From here it's southwest for a level stretch with views to the village of Zoza and red crests beyond. A lane lined with giant fennel plants leads past old houses and a cemetery crowded with monumental family tombs. Turn left for the 'source' (spring), and close-by amidst the scent of lime trees is the church of sleepy hamlet

2hr – Altagène (650m). No facilities, apart from a public phone.

Go past the telephone booth beneath a huge walnut tree for the overgrown track left. A road is joined then you drop via houses to an old church (Sant'Andrea). More road crossing and flights of steps follow, as the red rooftops ahead get closer. Once down amongst the houses, turn right for the marvellous fountain in the main square, Place des Monuments aux Morts, belonging to picturesque

40min – Ste Lucie de Tallano (450m) aka Santa Lucia di Tallà. Cafés with scenic terraces, eateries, grocery shops, bus. The *gîte d'étape* is a signposted 200-metre stroll away. ☎ 04 95788256, sleeps 30, open April to mid-October. It occupies a beautifully restored building close to a traditional 18th-century olive mill that is open for visits.

   The town name Tallano is believed to derive either from the Arabic for 'gift of Allah' or the Corsican for 'steep hillside'. As well as a number of churches and the derelict 15th-century convent of St François that affords lovely views over the town, it is famous for the rare stone *diorite orbiculaire*, a curious blue-grey with lighter concentric rings, used for the Medici chapel in Florence. Funnily enough the Corsicans call it the 'eye stone', while the town's revered namesake St Lucy (of Syracuse) is the patron saint of the blind.

DAY 5: STE LUCIE DE TALLANO TO PROPRIANO
(total 6hr 45min, 21.3km/13.3 miles, ascent/descent 670m/1120m)

Leave the *gîte* on a path past the olive press to join the quiet road heading right (northwest) for the houses of **Poggio**. You then drop through extensive olive groves

Some wild landscapes and plenty of strenuous walking as the route drops to the coast.

*Romanesque church
of St Jean Baptiste*

and coast past the derelict Romanesque church of St Jean Baptiste. A track is crossed and a path (keep an eye out for waymarks) leads through a wood of broom and cork oaks in various stages of 'undress'. Down at the Rivière Rizzanese, the path follows the banks before encountering the

1hr – Pont de Piombatu (120m), a favourite spot for fishermen, where two pretty cascading watercourses join forces. Signs forbid bathing due to dangerous currents.

A lane heads uphill tending north through light evergreen oak woods, to the D69, a short distance below Loreto de Tallano. Keep left and take the signed lane through to a series of farm buildings and rusting machinery (Maddalena). Waymarking disappears briefly but you need the tarmac road uphill past warning signs related to quarry work. A marked path with cairns soon breaks off right into dense old woods maintaining a constant south-westerly direction, climbing steadily to a rock gully bright with lilac-pink stonecrop. You may come face to face with the odd sheep crashing through the undergrowth of bracken and brambles. The route eventually reaches

1hr 30min – Punta d'Arja Vecchia col (600m) with a ruined hut. Marvellous views take in nearby Pointe de Zibo, the river and farming plain below and the distant Bavella zone.

A further modest climb leads along a wild open crest smothered in heady scented lavender, cistus and pungent herbs. The low maquis vegetation means chances are good of seeing buzzards and argumentative crows. Around 700m in altitude beneath a prominent elongated rock outcrop the way levels out and flanks an old stone wall, one of the many criss-crossing the hillside. Chaotic scratchy shrubs have invaded the path making the going tiring, so shift to the wider parallel track as soon as a way through presents itself.

At a track junction, keep right (north-northwest) around the hillside, in gentle descent across arid open terrain. After a wire gate, the village of Arbellara comes into sight, backed by the glittering sea at last! Waymarking is more plentiful on the ensuing downhill amble below a modest farm then on a narrow path through shoulder high thistles you cruise into pretty

1hr 30min – Fozzano (400m) looking out west over the Gulf de Valinco. Historic towers, well-stocked grocery store, café. The village is famous as the home of Colomba, unforgiving 18th-century figure enmeshed in a terrible story of typical vendetta killings, whose story was adapted by French novelist Mérimée. Another infamous native son, a wealthy count, made a deal with the devil to guard his fabulous treasure while he fought off the Moors, and offered him a hundred souls as a reward.

An unofficial but well-used **variant** that drops southwest from the village means cutting out 4km of tarmac below, though the disadvantages it entails are a monotonous 6km dirt track with very little shade. Leave the village via the cemetery on a dusty farm track down the dry hillsides to join the D557 where it's 3km west to Baracci and the main N196. Allow 2hr in all.

Via a ramp above a drinking fountain you take the road in the direction of Figaniella, breaking off left on the marked path between houses. Head west and after stream crossing it's mostly level going around to a panoramic outcrop. The path then shifts northwest descending gradually through a wood to a further watercourse, then the Rivière de Baracci, with an old mill.

A final easy climb through thick forest which echoes with cuckoo cries, brings you out on the D557 at San Quircu on the valley floor. Turn left for the short distance to the tiny rural settlement of

1hr 15min – Burgo (190m) and its helpful and friendly *gîte* U Fracintu ☎ 04 95761505, sleeps 95, open year-round. From here it's 7km into Propriano, and the meagre alternatives are a slog on foot along the surfaced road (about 1hr 30min) or an attempt at hitchhiking.

The quiet road along the Baracci valley passes a low-key spa zone and finally a horse-riding centre-cum-*gîte* at Baracci (☎ 04 95761948, open year-round) just before the main road N196, 2.5km northeast of

Propriano, renowned for plentiful accommodation and traffic jams, is good for a swim and a well-earned cool beer. Banks, shops of all kinds and bus services. ① 04 95760149. Loft Hotel ☎ 04 95761748.

SHORT WALKS

1: St-Florent Coastal Route

Walking time	4hr
Distance	16.8km/10.4 miles
Difficulty	Grade 1
Map	IGN scale 1:25,000 sheet 4348OT
Start/Finish	marina car park at St-Florent

A string of divine white sand beaches fringing secluded coves with inviting Caribbean-coloured water is encountered on this glorious coastline ramble. An especially peaceful route, accessible only to walkers and boaters in the absence of a road, it belongs to the Nebbio region, whose name derives from the dense moisture-bearing mists that envelop it in late winter and autumn. These encourage the vineyards on the fertile hilly hinterland of St-Florent which produce some of the island's best wine, Patrimonio. In striking contrast is the arid neighbouring Désert des Agriates. This hostile spread, unusually bare and infertile for Corsican standards, was supposedly devastated by the long-standing war between a couple of proud counts in the Middle Ages. The Almighty decreed nothing should grow in the desert-like area to testify to their absurd childish rivalry.

Commencing at the pretty port and haven of St-Florent, the walk itself has negligible ascent and descent, and entails a lovely ramble from turquoise bay to turquoise bay backed by modest arid hills as it heads along the eastern edge of the so-called desert. It can easily be done in sandals with a good grip, in preference to hot, sweaty boots. Beach gear including a mask or goggles will be appreciated, as will drinks, a picnic and sun protection. In addition, binoculars will enhance observation of both birds of prey and marine types. ▶

A worthwhile **extension**: from Santu beach, the destination of this walk, an extra 45min brings you to a remarkable watchtower on Punta Mortella, then it is a further 1hr to Loto beach. Here local craft ferry passengers to and from St-Florent in summer, a novel and relaxing way to go back. In all this means approximately the same total walking time, as you're saved the return stretch. Remember to check the last ferry time at the St-Florent marina before setting out.

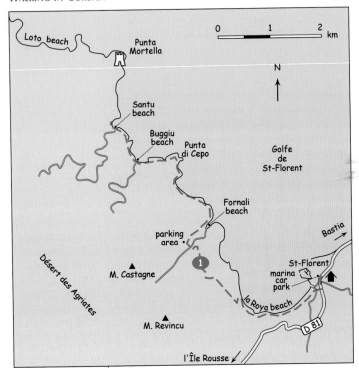

Some historic trivia: the landmark watchtower at Punta Mortella was erected in 1520 by the Genoese authorities to counter the devastating pirate incursions along the vulnerable coastline. Later on, when Corsica was annexed by France, the English were bent on destroying as many watchtowers as possible in revenge for the death of Nelson at Trafalgar. But it took them a full week in 1794 to break down the defences at Punta Mortella. So impressed were they with the multistoreyed design that they copied it for a string of similar structures along the southeast coast of England and Ireland during the Napoleonic wars. They renamed them the Martello Towers, inspired by the Italian for 'hammer', and numerous exemplars still standing continue their vigil.

The start point, the picturesque town of St-Florent, is set in a quiet cul-de-sac on the eponymous gulf. Though understandably touristy, it has retained its small-scale feel and can still be cosy at non-peak times. Dominated by a photogenic citadel, it offers attractive waterside seafood restaurants and a good range of accommodation, including campsites. Visitors who happen to be around on 2 June will witness the colourful feast of St Erasmus, patron saint and protector of sailors as well as people suffering from intestinal disorders. Accompanied by local dignitaries, his beneficent statue is borne around the harbour to bless the waters and fishing fleet amidst a honking flotilla, and a wreath is cast into the bay. 1 May, on the other hand, is the day to drop in on Saint Flora entombed in the cathedral. Follow the devout to a hole in the northern wall from which the scent of violets emanates just for the occasion. ▶

Facilities: ① 04 95370604. Of the many accommodation options, Hotel du Centre ☎ 04 95370068, true to its name, is located a mere stone's throw from the marina and seafront, where all the action is.

Access: St-Florent can be reached by buses from and to Bastia except Sundays and holidays, all times of year,

St-Florent

and from Calvi in summer. Those travelling by car will need the D81 that crosses from Bastia over to the west coast and l'Île Rousse.

From the **car park** at St-Florent's marina start out on the D81 signed for l'Île Rousse. After a couple of minutes' walking inland leave the road for the footbridge right (west) over the Aliso watercourse. It's not far to where straggly tamarisk line the first stretch of the family beach **la Roya**, backed by holiday apartments and a camping ground. Fluffy brown balls of *Posidonia oceanica* seaweed are scattered over the sand. Looming inland to the west is the gentle slope of M. Revincu. At the far end of the beach turn left on a minor road which quickly veers right and becomes a dusty track. As a eucalypt-lined avenue it passes rural properties complete with olive groves, before swinging northwest over a hill to traverse a side valley in the shade of low-lying M. Castagne. Stay with it until a branch right to a ruined hut and rough **parking area**, along with a faint sign for the 'Chemin du Littoral'.

Dark blue paint splashes point the way through light scrub to the pretty if tiny **Fornali** beach (1hr), with lovely views over the gulf to the rugged mountains of Cap Corse. Now you proceed essentially northwards, close to the water's edge, in and out of a delightful succession of tiny beaches and inviting rocky inlets below several houses. Take care to close gates behind you and respect the 'private property' signs. Waist-high evergreen shrubs, flag-like ferulas and woolly yellow everlasting accompany the path, not to mention the riot of crimson and purple from stonecrop and gladiolus. Stone markers with arrows show the way at forks.

After rounding Punta di Cepo, a stretch due west ends with a brief climb over a rise to the glorious sandy stretch of **Buggiu** beach (40min). A generous strip of sand colonised by bright Hottentot fig flowers and possibly cows separates the sea from a rush-filled pond, actually the termination of a watercourse of the same name. A further easy 20min on is yet another lovely bay and beach, **Santu** (total 2hr), popular with boat-borne locals. ◀

Extension: The path to Punta Mortella and Loto continues northwards hugging the coastline – an extra 1hr 45min should be allowed.

Return to **St-Florent** along the same paths (2hr). In all likelihood it will take you much longer as you try out the different swimming spots.

Buggiu beach

2: The Fango Valley

Walking time	2hr 30min
Distance	3.8km/2.4 miles
Difficulty	Grade 1
Map	IGN scale 1:25,000 sheet 4149OT
Start/Finish	Ponte Vechju

A bed of warm orange-red porphyry rock scooped out over the ages into smooth basins by the flow of snowmelt from the far-off peaks around the Paglia Orba – this is the River Fango, a tongue-in-cheek denomination, perhaps, as the name means 'mud'! Its valley receives surprisingly few visitors, apart from long-distance walkers on the Mare e Monti route. A straightforward path strolls along

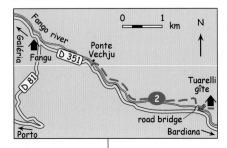

the banks of the watercourse punctuated by crystal-clear rock pools and gentle cascades. There is little in the way of ups and downs, making it suitable for all members of the family.

All around are immense hillsides cloaked by a massive forest of Mediterranean oaks, purportedly the most extensive in the whole of Europe. Another attraction comes in the form of a classical, gracefully arched Genoese bridge, the Ponte Vechju, beautifully restored to its former elegance. The destination on the other hand is a simple walker's hostel-cum-café/eatery in the isolated hamlet of Tuarelli not far upstream. The river flow is much deeper and more dramatic here. A shady terrace overlooks more rock pools and cascades to explore, so don't forget your swimming gear, as a dip in the invigorating river water is unbeatable on a scorching hot Corsican summer's day. ◀

Facilities: Tuarelli camping ground, café/restaurant and *gîte* ☎ 04 9562 0175, sleeps 24, open April to October. Otherwise a restaurant operates in summertime at Ponte Vechju, while a matter of kilometres back towards the coast there are snack bars and hotels at Fangu, including family-run Hotel a Farera (also known as Chez Zeze) ☎ 04 95620187. B&B La Casaloha ☎04 95344695 lacasaloha@gmail.com

Access: 7km inland from Galéria on the D81, turn off at the straggle of buildings that go by the name of Fangu. Then you're on the minor road D351 for the final 1.5km to the Ponte Vechju footbridge, the walk start. If you have the use of two cars leave one at the arrival point, Tuarelli, though it's no great hardship returning on foot. If you have time to spare, drive further inland towards Bardiana following the course of the river for yet more scenic lookout points and river access.

Buses are few and far between: Tuarelli and neighbouring hamlets have school services, otherwise the summer line between Porto and Calvi will drop you off at the hamlet of Fangu, a mere 1.5km away.

Park on the side of the road in the vicinity of the restaurant then go left onto a lane for the **Ponte Vechju** (46m). The lovely Genoese bridge spans the River Fango at an impressive height, over brilliant clear water. It was constructed directly onto the uneven rock base with masonry supports of notably differing heights. At the end of the parapet on the opposite bank, a narrow path turns down right. Higher outcrops and pebbly beaches alternate along the route as you head southeast inland. A rainbow of coloured boulders are scattered along the banks dominated by the gentle slope of wooded hills. Further on the path moves through scratchy dry maquis dominated by myrtle shrubs alongside papery pink and white rock roses. Overgrown in parts the path runs alongside old stone walls delimiting poor pasture for the odd cow.

Red rock in the Fango river, with Ponte Vechju in the background

When you emerge on a farm road, turn right back towards the Fango river past simple stone houses amidst pretty rose gardens. Another high if not historic **road bridge** spans the deep green river as it flows through a veritable gorge between tall smooth cliffs frequented by high diving swifts. Don't cross over but keep left following signs for the *gîte d'étape*. A right turn at the next fork puts you on a quiet dirt lane parallel to the watercourse. It's not far to the camping ground and the **Tuarelli *gîte*** (1hr 15min, 90m). Out of sight at first, it boasts a lovely terrace shaded by old olive trees and overlooking divine natural swimming pools. By all means take the plunge straightaway and wade upstream to explore the higher pools. Then enjoy a cool drink or meal.

Go back to the start point **Ponte Vechju** the same way (1hr 15min), unless you prefer taking the quiet road. In this case, cross the road bridge at Tuarelli and turn right towards the coast.

3: Visiting Girolata

Walking time	3hr 15min
Distance	10.2km/6.3 miles
Difficulty	Grade 1–2
Ascent/descent	420m/420m
Map	IGN scale 1:25,000 sheet 4149OT
Start/Finish	Bocca a Croce

The Scandola promontory and Girolata

Girolata is a picturesque isolated hamlet of hardy fishing folk. Protected by a providential promontory and set on a romantic cove in the broad sweep of the eponymous gulf, it feels like it's miles from anywhere. In fact it is accessible

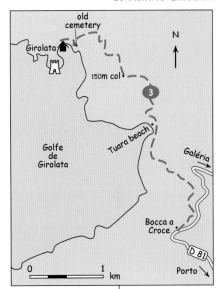

exclusively by boat or on foot. Girolata lies some 300m below the remarkably scenic road that snakes its harrowing way along the island's west coast. The settlement comes complete with one of the ubiquitous fortified Genoese towers that dot the Corsican coast. It testifies to the turbulent past when Corsairs dropped in to raid on a regular basis, occasionally repulsed when the Genoese and the likes of Admiral Andrea Doria ruled the seas and protected their interests. Nowadays the tower-castle is a private residence, while Girolata itself is home to an easygoing band of fishermen who supply the summer restaurants and visiting yachts with fresh seafood – lobsters included – when they're not ferrying visitors around the beautiful headland occupied by the renowned Scandola Reserve next door.

Created in 1975 and since recognised by UNESCO as a World Heritage site, Scandola embraces 1000 hectares of sea and 919 hectares of inaccessible igneous rock headland peaking at 560m above sea level. Out of bounds to walkers, it is thickly carpeted with woody shrub vegetation typical of the Mediterranean maquis, and harbours a rare type of armeria or thrift. Offshore the unusually transparent waters encourage the growth of vast dense beds of the seaweed *Posidonia oceanica*, not to mention fish and lobsters. The land part is inhabited by horned goat-like mouflon, and doubles as a breeding ground or stopover for migratory birds including shags, osprey, the peregrine falcon and reputedly even the massive bearded vulture.

The walk itself follows the track used by the trusty postman (alias 'Guy Le Facteur') and makes for a lovely

Facilities: A delightful option for the walk is to spend a night at Girolata, but do phone ahead to assure yourself a bed and evening meal at one of the waterfront *gîtes d'étape*: La Cabane du Berger (☎ 04 95201698, sleeps 30, open April to end September) or Le Cormoran Voyageur (☎ 04 95201555, sleeps 20, open April to end September).

day out. A swim or two is feasible, as is either a fish lunch on the terrace of one of the rustic (though not cheap) restaurants or a self-made picnic.

The walk start, Bocca a Croce or Col de la Croix, is a modest saddle on the neck of the promontory of Capo Senino. It is one of the few plausible – not to mention compulsory – stopping points on the tortuous road. It has cramped roadside parking and a snack bar or two. Most importantly Bocca a Croce is a prime viewing spot for admiring the red rocks and sweep of the gulf to Scandola, backed by a succession of headlands. ◀

Access: Bocca a Croce is approximately equidistant between Galéria and Porto on the D81. It is served by a bus between Porto and Calvi from May to October.

Having enjoyed the stunning views, leave **Bocca a Croce** (269m) on the clear path in steady descent northwards shaded by Mediterranean oaks. Plenty of rock rose shrubs harbour curious egg-like yellow-red parasite plants at their base. A drinking fountain is passed about halfway down. The track emerges at **Tuara** beach (30min), a decent stretch of sand between orange-hued volcanic-looking rocks. It is strewn with dried seaweed strands and probably occupied by lazing cows.

At the far end of the beach, a little way inland you'll find a path heading uphill north once more. A short slog brings you to a signed junction at a **col** (150m). Turn left to join the main Mare e Monti long-distance route for the final stretch of descent. Bearing northwest through shady tall scrub, you follow a dry stone wall. A lovely outcrop overlooking the bay is the site for the tiny **old cemetery**. Then it's down to sea level, where a footbridge traverses a stream amidst a riot of showy yellow horned poppies and joins the shingle beach of **Girolata** (1hr).

Directly opposite the jetties – umbilical cords for landing essential supplies for the community – is the first restaurant-cum-*gîte d'étape*, set back a little in the shade of eucalypts. A little further on, past the diminutive grocery store, is the second hostel, overlooking the bay.

Above it amidst laden fig and olive trees are more eateries and the mighty Genoese tower-cum-fortress.

Yellow horned poppies at Girolata

Time permitting, wander northwest along the high coast path towards the warm red rocks of the Scandola reserve. For the return to **Bocca a Croce** (269m), allow a total of 1hr 45min the same way back.

4: Spelunca Gorge

Walking time	2hr (3hr 30min from Ota)
Distance	4.1km/2.5 miles
Difficulty	Grade 1
Map	IGN scale 1:25,000 sheet 4250OT
Start/Finish	roadside parking above the Pont Génois

This is a popular route along the lovely Spelunca river gorge, so don't expect to enjoy it in solitude in high season. It's not exactly a canyon, and lacks the dramatic earthy colours of the Fango river, but does have a special

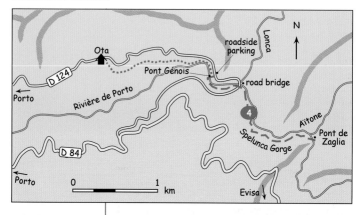

Extension: The walk can be extended by continuing on past the second bridge, Pont de Zaglia, and embarking on the stiff climb for the scenically placed village of Evisa, as per the long-distance Mare e Monti route, Day 8. But remember to allow extra time for the return.

charm of its own. This is created by a combination of elegant historic stone bridges and dense vegetation, which on the one hand embraces a riot of wild flowers but on the other tends to obscure views of the watercourses and surrounding mountains. A relaxing day can easily be spent here bathing in the rock pools and picnicking, so go prepared with swimming gear, drinks and food. ◀

A curiosity: at the rear of Ota is the modest mountain Capu d'Ota (not to be confused with outstanding Capu d'Ortu southwest), its position apparently a threat to the houses. However, the locals have no fears on this score, as they believe the mountain to be anchored in place by three strong chains of a celestial nature.

Access: Approaching from Porto, take the winding D84 inland for 7.5km then fork down left to the river side. Just after the road bridge park at the signpost for the Pont Génois/Pont Vecchiu. Otherwise take the even narrower D124 via Ota and continue down to the river that way. By public transport, catch the bus from Porto to Ota.

From the village, follow the orange paint splashes for the long-distance route Mare e Monti. Past Chez Félix restaurant it follows lanes down below the road to the Pont Génois (Genoese bridge), a descent of 120m. This means an extra 1hr 30min including the return, so a grand total of 3hr 30min for the walk.

From the **roadside parking**, hunt out the wooden sign pointing towards the river and the bridge. It's a short shady way down to the graceful stone structure of **Pont Génois**, also known as Ponte Vecchiu or 'old bridge' (200m). Dating back to the 14th–15th century period of Genoese domination, it has since been beautifully restored and is reputedly the most outstanding exemplar of its kind on the island. Moreover, at its foot is inviting clear green water and lovely swimming spots accessible from the low banks of the Rivière de Porto.

On the opposite bank a signed path turns left over rough terrain. It quickly improves, and as a wide track leads past playing grounds to the **road bridge**. This marks the confluence of the Lonca and the Aïtone, which you now proceed to follow up its right bank, as signposted for Evisa.

A delightful path rambles along the watercourse, gradually squeezed between higher grey cliffs. Old stone walls and myriad wild flowers and shrubs line the way, from foxgloves to Corsican hellebore, cyclamens, tongue orchids

Facilities: Ota has two well-used *gîtes d'étape*: Chez Marie ☎ 04 95261137, sleeps 30, open year-round, and Chez Félix ☎ 04 95261292, sleeps 50, open year-round, while the coastal resort of Porto ⓘ 04 95261055 has plenty of hotels, camping grounds and a well-stocked supermarket.

Magnificent Genoese bridge on the Spelunca walk

and rock roses. Further on, through a tangle of vegetation your destination, moss-ridden **Pont de Zaglia** (280m, 1hr) appears at the point where the renowned Aïtone and Tavulella flow together. Ducking in and out of scented green alder shrubs, paths fan out from here to explore the two streams with more swimming and lunch spots.

Return the same way to the **Pont Génois** and start point (a further 1hr).

5: A Calanche Walk

Walking time	1hr
Distance	3.2km/2 miles
Difficulty	Grade 1–2
Ascent/descent	100m/100m
Map	IGN scale 1:25,000 sheet 4150OT
Start/Finish	Les Roches Bleues kiosk

'After passing through Piana, I unexpectedly entered a fantastic forest of pink granite, a forest of peaks, columns, astonishing shapes, gnawed at by time, by the rain, by the winds, by the salt-ridden spray of the sea… You could make out crouching lions, robed monks, bishops, ghastly devils, inordinately large birds, portentous creatures, a haunting nightmarish menagerie.'

Guy de Maupassant, 1881

According to murky local stories, this landscape was the fantastic work of the devil in order to frighten a young shepherdess who dared to turn him down.

The Calanche are a precious pocket of dramatic rock-scapes and plunging cliffs, making for wonderful scenery and duly recognised and protected by UNESCO as a World Heritage site. Most visitors are content to admire them from road level, but this short walk will give you the feeling of entering right into the landscape and give you the chance to appreciate its marvellous oddities. There

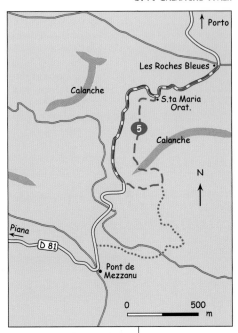

are wonderful contrasts – pink-red rocks, deep blue sea and hopefully a cloudless sky.

The walk itself, but one of the network through the Calanche and the Forêt Communale de Piana, wends its way through a petrified forest of rock spires and weird stone shapes which assume warming rosy-orange hues especially towards sunset, thanks to their granite-porphyry blend. What's more, the quiet path affords stunning views over a long stretch of the wild western coast of Corsica, and the vegetation, as usual, is unexpectedly abundant – notably pretty yellow domes of dwarf broom. It used to be part of the mule track that extended past Piana to link up with the isolated villages of Porto and Ota. The road was not constructed until 1850, under Napoleon III. ▶

Access: Running down the mid-western coast of Corsica, the sinuous D81 links the villages of Piana and Porto. There is a year-round bus link from Ajaccio via Cargèse to Piana, whence Porto. The start point, Les Roches Bleues kiosk, is about 4km from Piana and 7km from Porto. Limited car parking is possible in the vicinity, otherwise you may be able to squeeze in at the roadside where the actual path starts.

From the tongue-in-cheek named **Les Roches Bleues** (428m) café and its marvellous position, walk southwest

Facilities: The nearest accommodation is at Piana, Hôtel Mare e Monti ☎ 04 9527 8214, ① 04 9527 8442 (summer only).

for 5min along the road in the direction of Piana to a prominent rock which sports a madonna statue in a niche (S.ta Maria Orat.). Here a track signed 'ancien chemin' turns uphill (blue waymarking), the erstwhile main route between Piana and Ota. Accompanied by flowering red valerian, easy but decisive zigzags lead to a minor pass (520m), where you unexpectedly emerge to find yourself above the calanche shapes. The views are obviously stunning and range north across the bay to Capo Senino, backed by the sweep of rugged coastline up towards the Golfe de Girolata.

The clear rock path continues south high above the road and widens into a recognisable mule track. All around is a veritable rock garden, where bright purple stonecrop and yellow broom have somehow found a foothold on the rough granite surface and double as hiding places for lightning-fast lizards. The village of Piana comes

At Les Roches Bleues kiosk in the Calanche

into view southwest as you move around to a beautifully restored stretch of track with dry-stone reinforcement.

Lilac orchid-like limodores appear as the path enters light wood. A couple of minutes in, you leave the good path for a rougher goat track (right) that drops to the road through shrubs. Watch your step, as the loose stones don't work wonders for the ankles. ▶

Back down at the road, turn right for the short return to Les Roches Bleues, and be specially careful of oncoming traffic at the blind curves.

6: Capu Rossu

Walking time	3hr (5hr 20min from Piana)
Distance	6.3km/3.9 miles
Difficulty	Grade 2
Ascent/descent	530m/530m
Map	IGN scale 1:25,000 sheet 4150OT
Start/Finish	roadside kiosk

This is a hard walk to beat in Corsica. Capu Rossu (or Capo Rosso) is a spectacular headland jutting out into the turquoise Mediterranean Sea a short distance from the Calanche village of Piana. It is evidently the most westerly landpoint of the whole island (unless you count the minuscule islands just off the Scandola promontory), and spells amazing all-round views. As might be expected, it is the site of a masterly watchtower dating back to Genoese times, namely 14th–15th century, and now protected under the auspices of UNESCO. It is accessible for visitors – those who still have the energy to ascend it after the arduous climb.

As the headland is exposed to the elements, the walk is inadvisable in bad weather or when strong winds could pose danger. On the other hand, in blinding sunshine sunscreen and a broad-rimmed hat are essential as there is no

Extension (extra 30min): instead of dropping to the road via the goat track, it is possible to proceed on the good path. It continues southwards, and eventually passes playing grounds before joining the D81 close to the Pont de Mezzanu. Either turn right here for Les Roches Bleues or go left for the remaining 1.5 km to Piana.

shade at all. Try to avoid the climb in the midday heat, though the chances are usually good of a cooling sea breeze. Trainers could be used, but light-weight boots with ankle support are preferable as the paths are rife with loose stumbling stones. Abundant drinking water is another must. At walk's start and end, the laid-back kiosk, provides cool drinks on a welcome shady platform. ◀

Facilities: Peaceful Piana ① 04 9527 8442 (summer only) is a good base for visiting this region. It has a good range of shops, restaurants, miscellaneous services and accommodation including Hôtel Mare e Monti ☎ 04 95278214.

Access: The year-round bus service operates along the main coast road D81 between Ajaccio and Porto and passes through Piana. The walk start is a further 6km out of town on the narrow D824 that drops to the beach of Arone. After a high scenic stretch as the road veers left (south) in descent, pull off at the corner for the kiosk and adjacent parking area. Anyone approaching on foot from Piana (if hitching doesn't work or there are no taxis available) should allow a little over 1hr either way.

Those arriving on foot from Piana will encounter a sign-post for the 'Tour de Capu Rossu' a little before the **roadside kiosk** (319m). Heading off due west it is quickly joined by the path from the car park. Marked with red paint splashes, it makes its way across open maquis and a riot of cistus and glittery purple-pink stonecrop. Right from the word go the red hump of Capu Rossu topped by its trademark tower is ahead of you, a tempting and attractive destination – if a little distant. The path cuts across an easy slope, while hidden from sight for the moment is a sheer drop to the sea only a short way to your right! Accompanied by scented rosemary and aromatic everlasting, you head steadily downhill through old enclosures for livestock, the hillside dotted with abandoned stone herders' huts. Below is the divine blue sea.

The walk's halfway point in terms of timing is a modest **shepherd's hut** (60m), where you veer right (northwest) and uphill for a climb over bright red rock colonised with a remarkable array of flowering plants, such as scented pinks. A shallow gully leads up a plateau, where heaped stone cairns guide you towards the lookout tower Tour de Turghiu and its awe-inspiring location. This is **Capu Rossu** (1hr 30min, 331m), where breathtaking cliffs edged with thorny yellow blooms plunge to pretty rocky coves where leisure craft hang suspended over brilliant turquoise water. Views range way back into the mountainous interior as well as for miles both ways along the rugged coast, taking in the Golfe de Porto and Scandola promontory to the north. The tower is always open and steps lead up to the roof terrace, where you join the skylarks on top of the world, the sea at your feet.

Return to the **roadside kiosk** the same way (same timing).

Watchtower on Capu Rossu

7: The Aïtone Forest and Rock Pools

Walking time	2hr 30min
Distance	8km/5 miles
Difficulty	Grade 1–2
Ascent/descent	182m/182m
Map	IGN scale 1:25,000 sheet 4150OT
Start/Finish	Evisa

A stone's throw inland from Porto on the beautiful west coast, the renowned Aïtone forest of towering Corsican and maritime pines is watered by a picture-postcard river that cascades around granite boulders, forming inviting pools. A further attraction is the swaying suspension bridge, a short wander upstream.

Guy de Maupassant travelled this way on horse-back in 1880, though his impressions of the forest are a little chilling:

> 'The way climbed gently in the middle of the forest of Aïtone. The monstrous pine trees spread a groaning vault overhead, with a sort of unceasing sad lament, to both the right and left their slender straight trunks formed an army of organ pipes that seemed to emit this monotonous music of wind in the tree tops'.

The start point, Evisa, is a pretty mountain village with crisp cool air, worlds away from the beaches. Its streets lined with scented lime trees offer wonderful views over rugged valleys and soaring peaks such as mighty Capu d'Ortu, west-southwest.

The straightforward walk climbs out of the village on a gentle gradient through shady chestnut woods to the forest itself and watercourse. A dip in the invigorating water is welcome in the heat of the summer, but only for the hardy, otherwise you'll probably be content with a picnic in this magical place. This is an extremely popular spot, but paths lead off right, left and centre

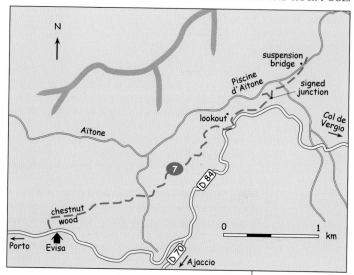

around the pools and along the torrent, so it's not hard to find a place to yourself even in peak season. Take care with young children as the rocks around the pools can be slippery.

Variants: The walk can be shortened by 1hr 30min if you start out at the parking area on the D84 higher up. On the other hand a feasible extension – entailing a further 45min and 200m uphill – on a steep path through some great rock and forest landscapes takes you to more rock pools at Pont Casterica (see Mare-Mare Nord, Day 3). From there, as an alternative to backtracking, you can branch right (east) for the D84 road and try your luck at catching a lift for the 6.5km back to Evisa.

Access: Inland Evisa has a year-round bus to Ajaccio, while a summer line goes to Corte and Porto. By car

Facilities: Evisa is a lovely spot for a meal or overnight stay, and has grocery shops and several hotels, such as U Pozzu ☎ 04 95262289, open April–October, as well as a popular *gîte d'étape* ☎ 04 95262188, sleeps 37, open April to mid-October.

there's the panoramic D84 from near Corte via Col de Vergio and on to Porto, or the minor D70, a relatively direct route from Ajaccio.

In the main street of **Evisa** (850m) beset with chattering swifts, let your nose lead you to the *boulangerie* (bakery). Directly opposite, a concrete ramp and flight of steps signed 'le Chemin des Châtaigniers' heads uphill and past a Mare-Mare Nord board for the start of an old pretty track through an age-old chestnut woods. A series of helpful panels explains the traditional methods for gathering, drying and milling. Opposite are pig sties, though the majority of the inmates will be encountered wandering through the woods on their foraging expeditions.

Hemmed in by dry-stone walls, the old paved lane dips across a stream and negotiates a mud-ridden stretch then climbs gradually through a mix of dark Austrian pine and deciduous trees. It's not far up to where the road (**D84**) swings around to meet the track (car parking). Keep to the left side of the road, taking care not to miss the unmarked faint fork left between towering pines

Belvedere in the Aïtone forest

for an exciting **lookout** over the cascading Aïtone way below and scaly rock precipices opposite.

Back at the roadside, you'll soon need the broad lane branching down left accompanied by foxgloves through the magnificent wood, home to woodpeckers and cuckoos. After timber picnic benches is a **signed junction** for Col de Vergio. Yours is the left branch – high, knee-jarring giant steps down to the celebrated **Piscine d'Aïtone** (910m, 1hr). These brilliant if coolish rock pools are scattered along the cascading watercourse.

When you've had your fill return to the **signed junction** and go left for Col de Vergio as per the long-distance Mare-Mare Nord route. It crosses a moss-ridden side stream then becomes a narrow path high on the river bank. You soon reach a **suspension bridge** (970m, 15min). While not exactly Indiana Jones, its still fun to cross – one at a time though.

Unless you opt for the extension to 1170m Pont de Casterica (see above), make your way back to **Evisa** along the same path (1hr 15min).

8: The Paglia Orba Loop

Walking time	5hr (extra 40min from Hotel Castel de Vergio)
Distance	14km/8.7 miles
Difficulty	Grade 2
Ascent/descent	800m/800m
Map	IGN scale 1:25,000 sheet 4250OT
Start/Finish	Col de Vergio

This superb popular day route is set in the northwestern sector of Corsica's rocky central highlands, on the verge of the Niolo district, in the domain of the Paglia Orba, one of the loftiest mountains on the island. Showing a marked resemblance to a recumbent elephant when approached

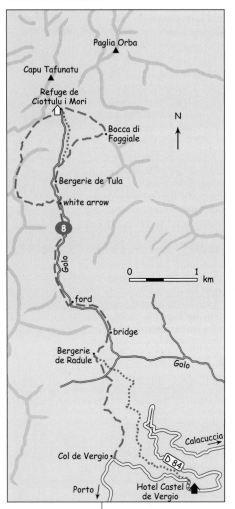

from the south, the peak is markedly different seen from paths on the west coast, its hook-shaped profile a constant presence on the horizon. Dorothy Carrington (1971) fills us in on the name 'Paglia Orba: the words are numinous to English ears, suggesting the opening, or refrain of an incantation, an orison to a divinity which is the peak itself, but in fact – in accordance with the realistic Corsican mind – merely means "curved straw"'.

On the other hand a dramatic legend appealing to the inhabitants' boundless imagination explains the shape of the neighbouring mountain Capu Tafunatu (literally 'pierced peak') in terms of the age-old struggle between good and evil, saints versus the devil. Up to no good, Lucifer in disguise approached Saint Martin who was tending his flocks and requested to be taken into his service. However the strong sulphurous odour he gave off aroused the suspicion of the saint, who dismissed the would-be shepherd. Lucifer's next trick ensnared the village chief in a bet to build a much-needed bridge for herders over the Golo river. The

Taking it easy on the Paglia Orba walk

devil, incognito, was to have it ready before dawn in return for a choice piece of land (or a soul, depending on which version is adhered to). A split second before the keystone was slotted in, St Martin won the day by releasing a crowing cock ahead of sun-up. Beaten and enraged, Lucifer hurled his hammer madly up towards the mountains where it smashed through the rock, shaping aptly named Capu Tafunatu.

The walk gives a taste of the exciting GR20 long-distance trail, rating as fairly strenuous though not particularly difficult on this stretch. Remember that the route can always be interrupted and steps retraced. Note that an impetuous watercourse is forded, and while under midsummer conditions this is merely a matter of a short jump, it could prove tricky after heavy rain. Take care but not risks. Picnic supplies and plenty of drinking water are needed (water is also available at the refuge), but whatever else, don't neglect to pack swimming gear and sun block – the path quickly leaves the shady wood behind. Its initial stretch passes stands of magnificent Corsican pines which have thankfully

Facilities: From the Col de Vergio start point, quarter of an hour east down the D84 road is Hotel Castel de Vergio (☎ 04 95480001, sleeps 80), a useful base for walks in the area, not to mention as an alternate start point as explained below. It caters almost exclusively to long-distance walkers as both the GR20 and Mare-Mare Nord transit here, and it is a good place to meet other pedestrian tourists. On the other hand there is the high-altitude Refuge de Ciottulu i Mori at the foot of the Paglia Orba. It sleeps 26 in bunk beds, and can be used for an overnight stay if you take your own bedding and food and plan on arriving fairly early to ensure a place.

escaped fires. They boast an average height of 30m, and the oldest are a staggering 300 years old. ◀

Access: The road pass Col de Vergio (or Col de Verghio) is easily reached via the D84 from Porto on the mid-west coast. Otherwise from Corte in the centre of the island, take the D18 then D84 via Calacuccia – a summer-only bus does this same route.

At **Col de Vergio** (1478m) a scenic yellow-marked path strikes out north through the odd pine and beech, coasting in and out of minor side valleys. After a drop via a stream (keep your eyes peeled for waymarks), there's a brief exposed stretch on rocky steps that lead quickly around to join a wider path, the GR20 (see alternate access, below). Not far on, huge rock slabs cross a dramatic rushing stream that serves the superbly sited photogenic tumble of stone huts and pens of the **Bergerie de Radule** (1470m, 40min).

Alternate access from Hotel Castel de Vergio (1hr)

This uses the red/white marked GR20 route which branches northwest off the road only a matter of metres uphill from the hotel (1400m). It picks its straightforward way through pretty wood featuring elegant silver birches and scented spurge, along with numerous wonderfully huge Corsican pines. Continuous ups and downs lead north, crossing minor streams and intersecting the Mare-Mare Nord path. You climb to a minor wooded ridge with a great view over to a waterfall before coasting northwest around the corner to the Bergerie de Radule (1470m), where the main route is joined.

A brief downhill clamber brings you to the rushing torrent Golo, at the narrow opening of a promising valley hedged in by soaring granite ridges. The watercourse needs crossing at this point (**bridge**, 1470m), and while the smoothed rock surface means easy access, it can be insidiously slippery and the current strong, so watch your step. A series of easy stone steps

then proceeds north-northwest through thinning pines, curving west across an easily negotiated tumble of fallen rocks, climbing steeply at times. The scenery here is particularly alpine in feeling. The stream is traversed once again at some delightful rock pools fed by tumbling cascades (**ford**, 1544m).

Both Capu Tafunatu and Paglia Orba are visible during the climb

Decidedly above the tree line the valley levels out considerably, and you find yourself strolling north below high granite crests and amidst fragrant green alder shrubs and a surprising array of bright blooms such as white-purple butterwort and pink thrift. Many more inviting rock pools are encountered. Ahead, separated by a marked notch pass at the valley head, the warm reddish outlines of Paglia Orba and Capu Tafunatu are clearly visible, even the shaded 12x17m slit hole in the latter. A rainbow of rocks spreads at their foot.

Some way up, at about 1700m, you leave the valley floor to turn sharp left (west), marked by a large **white arrow** painted on a prominent rock (the return loop joins up here).

Tight zigzags climb to a very scenic ridge, from where a vast series of snow-spattered peaks stretch out

Alternate exit:
Should the need
arise for a slightly
faster exit, take the
faint path that
plunges due south
down the steep rub-
ble slope directly
below the hut. It fol-
lows the valley and
stream, rejoining the
main route at some
prominent boulders
prior to the 1700m
white arrow referred
to above. In all this
route cuts a good
40min off the timing.

south, while west is the coast with the village of Piana and the Capu Rossu promontory, amongst others. The ground is smothered in lilac crocus flowers and ground-hugging thorny broom.

The path resumes its northerly direction for **Refuge de Ciottulu i Mori** (1991m, 2hr 40min this far), at the foot of the two giant peaks. Water is available, thanks to the source of the Golo close by. ◀

As per GR20 waymarking, continue east over a bare rise. In a short while the slit hole in Capu Tafunatu behind you becomes visible again. Curving almost imperceptibly southeast you easily reach **Bocca di Foggiale** (20min, 1962m). The surrounds are stark and patchy with snow at the start of the season. Views range down east to the Calacuccia dam and lake, preceded by the prominent rock columns of the Cinque Frati ('five monks'), described by Carrington (1971) as 'an ascending file of ragged spires like a procession of hoary beings climbing into the heavens'. Northeast is twin-pointed Capu Falu and a hint of the mass of Corsica's highest peak, M. Cintu, just out of view.

Leaving the GR20 route here, turn right (southwest) on a clear if unmarked path down the rubble-strewn mountainside. In the proximity of two enormous rectangular fallen boulders, you link up with the direct exit route from the Refuge. Follow the left-hand side of the stream via the evocative ruins of Bergerie de Tula (1720m), and soon afterwards cross back over the Golo at the **white arrow** (30min, 1700m) for the main route followed in ascent.

Allow a further 50min back down to the **Bergerie de Radule**, depending on how many swimming stops you indulge in, then 40min for **Col de Vergio**, where the walk started.

9: The Tavignano Bridge

Walking time	4hr 30min
Distance	12km/7.5 miles
Difficulty	Grade 1–2
Ascent/descent	400m/400m
Map	IGN scale 1:25,000 sheet 4250OT
Start/Finish	northwestern edge of Corte

An ancient paved mule track leads out of the historic town of Corte and into the wild Tavignano river valley, a delightful route full of surprises. Following a section of the long-distance trail Mare-Mare Nord, it gradually penetrates the profound V-cleft valley, whose upper reaches become a dramatic gorge. While it cannot boast the breathtaking high-altitude alpine beauty of the nearby Vallée Restonica, it is definitely worth a visit. One of the beauties of this popular and straightforward walk is its ease of access due to the proximity to the town; another is its suitability for families; and last but not least the fact that the valley has no road, and so has retained its wild natural atmosphere and can only be visited on foot or horseback. As well as the river valley itself, with its varied vegetation

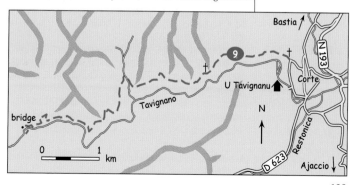

cover, a great attraction is the turn-around point, namely the bridge and rock pools, perfect for a refreshing, though chilly, dip.

Start walking as early as possible, especially in the heat of the summer, as you'll want to spend time at the river's edge, and remember to allow plenty of time for a leisurely return. Drinks and picnics as well as sun protection are essential, as no structures are encountered en route.

Further inspiration for the walk can be drawn from the widely held belief that this was the route taken by Napoleon's parents fleeing from Corte and the victorious French army over to the west coast. They travelled by mule, his mother well advanced in her expectant state with the great man.

If you feel up to it, continue past the bridge, as the further you go the more interesting and dramatic the gorge becomes, and the taller and straighter the magnificent Corsican pines – and the steeper and narrower the path! The higher area unfortunately bore the brunt of the extensive forest fires that ravaged the Corte region in the terrible summer of 2000. However, regrowth is amazingly rapid, and the park staff wasted no time in repairing the odd section of path damaged by falling trees and landslips.

Facilities: The university town of Corte, where the walk starts, has much to offer the visitor. A historic citadel, fine mountain views, good eating and the chance to hear some of the island's traditional unaccompanied singing, ⓘ 04 95462670. On the northern edge of town is the U Tavignanu family-run *gîte d'étape* and camping ground ☎ 04 95461685, sleeps 16, open year-round, book in advance. Otherwise in town itself is Hotel La Poste ☎ 04 95460137.

Note: Tempting Refuge A Sega is a further 3hr upvalley at 1190m. If you plan on an overnight stay there – a great idea – equip yourself with a sleeping bag. The recently inaugurated designer building, superbly set on the banks of the rushing river, has virtually everything – spacious dorm rooms, hot showers, hot meals and self-catering facilities, but no blankets. It's best to phone ahead to let them know you're coming: ☎ 04 95460790 (guardian's house at Corte – his wife takes the bookings and passes them on via radio) or mobile ☎ 06 10717726 (frequently no reception). Sleeps 36, open May–October. See the Mare-Mare Nord, Day 6, for path details. ◀

Access: Corte can easily be reached by both road and rail. There are rail links with Ajaccio, Bastia and Calvi, while coaches cover all points of the compass. By car the N193 is the major Bastia–Ajaccio artery.

The walk starts on the northwestern uppermost edge of Corte, close to the intersection of Rue St-Joseph and Chemin de Baliri, at the rear of the citadel – 10min on foot out of the town centre.

Leave **Corte** (420m) by the clear broad path signed for the Traversale Mare-Mare Nord and Refuge A Sega, and waymarked with orange paint stripes. Heading essentially east, it enters the broad mouth of the valley following the right bank of the Tavignano, the waters lazy and placid at this point. The ancient mule track passes a lovingly kept shrine and gains height very gradually. The surrounding terrain is rather dry at this point, colonised by typical maquis plants and rows of abandoned man-made terracing stretch out across the mountainsides.

After a second shrine there are light pine woods, then a miniature 'forest' of pretty white rock rose shrubs, joined by scented lavender. In a continual succession of brief ups and downs and old paved stretches, several side valleys with inviting rock pools are crossed. As the path nears the main valley, there are plunging views to the wild river bed as the gorge takes shape. Bizarrely shaped rock needles tower above the path. The vegetation soon includes trees such as the Mediterranean oak and tree heather, while the odd pine also makes its appearance.

The final stretch is virtually a shady stroll, and at the last minute you come across the **bridge** (760m, 2hr 30min). Take care clambering down to the rock pools. Anyone with the time and energy to proceed higher should expect a stiffer climb through a beautiful forest of towering Corsican pines that cover the left side of the river valley.

Return to **Corte** the same way you came, and allow 2hr from the bridge back to the road.

Artistic rock formations on the old Tavignano footpath

Artistic rock formations on the old Tavignano footpath

10: Glacial Lakes in the Restonica Valley

Walking time	3hr 30min
Distance	6km/3.7 miles
Difficulty	Grade 2–3
Ascent/descent	560m/560m
Map	IGN scale 1:25,000 sheet 4251OT
Start/Finish	Bergerie de Grottelle

A must-visit alpine valley of outstanding beauty only a short distance from the historic town of Corte in the island's mountainous centre, the Restonica has numerous attractions. These include a cluster of high-altitude

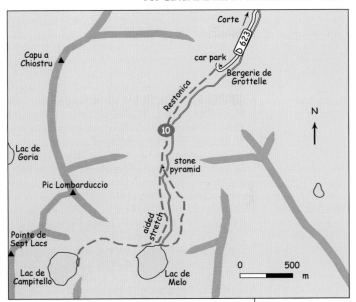

lakes set in cirques – basin-shaped depressions left by glacier action. The drive up the Restonica to the walk start is an experience in itself as the ever-narrowing road hugs the floor of the thickly forested valley, sticking close to the watercourse for the most part, which means that any number of wonderful rock pools with crystal-clear water cascading over bleached boulders are on hand for bathing, picnics or just lazing. In addition, outdoor eateries for all pockets, along with camping grounds, are strung along the valley.

There are a number of photogenically ramshackle stone huts still used by shepherds in the summer, but not usually until July, when temperatures are bearable for the livestock (and keepers) and there is enough pasture for feed. As regards other wildlife, the curly horned mouflon inhabits the rocky ridges well away from humans, while the magnificent bearded vulture is regularly reported gliding and patrolling rock faces for carrion – or succulent lambs, as the local herders would have it.

Remember that the walk start lies at an altitude of 1370m, so be prepared to don layers of warm clothing even if it's sweltering when you leave Corte. Moreover, don't do this walk until summer is well on the way if extensive snow cover bothers you. **Remember that this is high-altitude mountainous terrain, where unexpected changes in the weather can lead to dangerous situations.** An elementary climb – slippery in wet conditions – is involved en route to the first lake, though it can be avoided. In addition a couple of watercourses need crossing, tricky when the flow is impetuous. Carry food, drink and sun protection, as the path rises quickly above the tree line so there is no shade; this, combined with the altitude, requires a higher than usual factor sunscreen.

Due to the great appeal and popularity of the valley it gets very crowded, and each and every visitor needs to take special care not leave anything behind. Take all rubbish back to town where it can be disposed of properly. In mid-July the valley is the setting for an exciting race known as the Raid Inter-Lacs, which not only athletes will enjoy. ◀

Facilities: Restonica valley guesthouse Le Refuge: ☎ 04 95460913, sleeps 16, open April–October, 2km from the town centre. Corte ① 04 95462670.

Access: From Corte you need the well-signposted Restonica road, D623, south of town. Climbing some 900m in a southwesterly direction, the 16km road narrows considerably higher up, necessitating great caution. The upper section is usually closed to private vehicles in the peak July–September period, and a free shuttle service is provided from the last car park to the Bergerie de Grottelle.

As there is no public transport up the Restonica, carless visitors can either hire a taxi from Corte or try their hand at hitchhiking – a good bet as the traffic is mostly other walkers.

From the sizeable car park and friendly *buvette* (snack bar) above the picturesque huddle of stone shepherd's huts of the **Bergerie de Grottelle** (1370m), take the clear path

southwest marked with yellow paint splashes. Right from the start are great views of Capu a Chiostru and its grey rock points which dominates the scene on the way up, aided by adjacent rugged crests. A lovely waterfall is on the other side of the valley. Scattered pines line the way, but these soon give out due to the altitude, while scented green alder shrubs persist along the watercourse. Half an hour up, at a prominent **stone pyramid** on a modest plateau, keep right for the challenging partially aided route. (Otherwise keep left for the slightly longer path up the left-hand bank of the watercourse – used later in descent.)

You proceed over a series of rock slabs with the help of anchored chain and steps, entailing elementary hands-on climbing, with a little exposure. Once up at the level of lovely **Lac de Melo** (1hr, 1711m) in its steep-sided cirque, if you're not tempted to indulge in repose straightaway on the grassy picnic patches, turn right along its raised bank as far as a hut. Here, in view of the Pointe des Sept Lacs, the path for the next lake breaks off west, marked with yellow. A stiff climb ensues, and you emerge in a short corridor before bearing south for the last leg. After a modest rocky ridge you cross the outlet of

Capu a Chiostru dominates the upper Restonica valley

129

Lac de Campitello (1hr, 1930m), a marvellous spot. This is Corsica's fourth biggest lake, but its deepest at 42m, and it is home to salmon.

Time, energy and weather permitting, continue up a little further to get a bird's-eye view. In any case this is good spot to photograph the underlying lake. Of the surrounding mountains, pointed Pic Lombarduccio rises to the north, while south over the lake is towering Punta alle Porte. The long-distance route the GR20 passes on the ridge high above.

Retrace your steps the same way in descent to **Lac di Melo** (40min), then take the other more straightforward path in descent, after the aided route. Take care on the tricky stepping stones over the lake outlet stream, then

Lac de Melo in its glacial cirque

turn left for the steep rock steps that drop north on the right bank of the stream. This joins up with the ascent route in the vicinity of the **stone pyramid**.

Stick to the same route you climbed earlier on to return to the **Bergerie de Grottelle** (50min, 1370m).

11: La Cascade des Anglais

Walking time	2hr
Distance	7.3km/4.6 miles
Difficulty	Grade 1
Ascent/descent	350m/350m
Map	IGN scale 1:25,000 sheet 4251OT
Start/Finish	Vizzavona railway station

The 'English waterfall' walk spells stunning mountain scenery, magnificent Corsican pines and a delightful series of cascading falls over smoothed rock surfaces. The gentle climb on good paths makes this a perfect family walk with plenty of opportunities for lazing around, if not invigorating dips in the rock pools. It is understandably popular and has the added attraction of a modest snack bar close to the falls, handy for a coffee or snack.

The start point, Vizzavona, is essentially a scatter of buildings for a handful of permanent inhabitants (excluding hikers, the majority in summer) all but lost in a beautiful forest at 900m above sea level. Life centres around the diminutive station for the Ajaccio–Corte–Bastia railway line, which enters a long tunnel immediately uphill to save a final climb to the 1163m Col de Vizzavona. ▶

Facilities: Vizzavona has several restaurants, groceries and plenty of hiker's accommodation, including I Laricci ☎ 04 95472112, sleeps 36, open May–October.

Variant: A shorter track to the waterfalls leaves the main road at La Foce, close to the pass of Col de Vizzavona, heading west on a broad easy track.

131

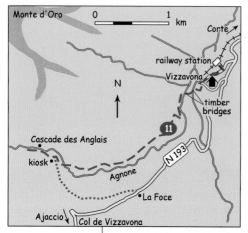

Access: As well as the train which runs year-round on a daily basis, Vizzavona can be reached by road on a brief detour from the N193 which dissects the island's central mountain range linking Bastia with Ajaccio.

Set out from the railway station at **Vizzavona** (910m) on the quiet signed road southish past the charming premises of the Hotel I Laricci. After a couple of bends, a path marked in red/white paint flashes breaks off right, in common with the long-distance GR20. Past a hut (Casa di a natura) where information on the forest is dispensed, it traverses a deliciously cool wood composed of a mix of conifers and deciduous trees and crosses two rustic **timber bridges**. An open stretch of forestry track featuring pretty purple orchids offers glimpses of the surrounding mountains, dominated by Monte d'Oro to the northwest. Soon a lovely wide path takes over, leading southwest through a beautiful thick beech wood, with cyclamens nestling in the undergrowth. Towering pines gradually take over, and spring visitors should look out for the endemic showy white lilies that thrive here.

Not far on you approach a footbridge over the gorge and emerald green rush of the Agnone. At the **kiosk** on the other side turn right for the short climb up the left bank to the **Cascade des Anglais** (1hr, 1250m) waterfall area at the foot of massive granite mountainsides punctuated with attractively weathered Corsican pines. The dozen or so cascades and pools are surrounded by attractive bleached rock, which offers inviting spots. Things improve with every step upwards, and though the

Cascade des Anglais

going gets rougher, it does become progressively quieter. (The path continues in ascent to a pasture zone and shepherd's hut.)

Return to **Vizzavona** the same way.

12: Trou de la Bombe

Walking time	2hr
Distance	6.1km/3.8 miles
Difficulty	Grade 1–2
Ascent/descent	100m/100m
Map	IGN scale 1:25,000 sheet 4253ET
Start/Finish	Col de Bavella

The Col de Bavella (or Bocca di Bavedda) road pass is one of the most stunning places in the whole of Corsica, thanks to the presence of a veritable army of weather-beaten Corsican pines set amongst bizarre granite

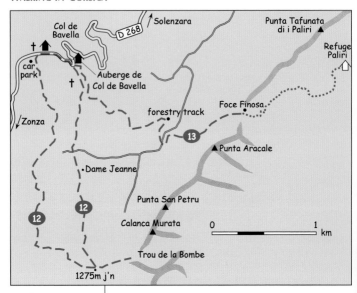

Facilities: There are two hotels-cum-*gîtes d'étape* at the pass as well as a grocery store: Auberge du Col de Bavella ☎ 04 95720987, sleeps 24, open April to early November, and Les Aiguilles de Bavella ☎ 04 9572018818, sleeps 18, open April to end October.

shapes and against the backdrop of the famous Aiguilles de Bavella rock needles. For Dorothy Carrington (1971) these were 'less suggestive of needles than a jawful of monster's teeth'! There also happen to be marvellous views down to the east coast. The pass has a distinctly alpine feel about it, with that crisp, dry feel in the air. Try to stay overnight there, as sunsets can be simply glorious, the slender pinnacles transformed into silhouettes of crimson and violet casting crazy long shadows over the thick forest.

This popular and straightforward circuit walk entailing a modest climb leads to a dramatic hole in a sheer rock face, Trou de la Bombe, which translates literally as 'bomb hole'! The afternoon is probably the best time to go, when the sun illuminates it from the front, enhancing photographs. As well as wonderful wild flowers such as tiny orchids, chances are good of glimpsing the native mouflon that inhabit this range. ◀

Access: Col de Bavella lies on the narrow winding D268 that zigzags up from Solenzara on the eastern coast, dropping to the village of Zonza after the pass. The Porto-Vecchio to Ajaccio bus includes an extension to Col de Bavella, but only during the midsummer months; otherwise get off at Zonza and try to hitch a lift the remaining 9km.

On the southern Zonza side of **Col de Bavella** (1218m), opposite the Notre Dame de la Neige shrine, an easy forestry track near the ample car park strikes out south-wards. It is marked with red paint and the odd low timber pole and signed for 'U Cumpuleddu', which corresponds to the recently revived Corsican appellation for Trou de la Bombe. Beneath towering pine trees with an undergrowth of foxgloves and dwarf broom, it advances in a southerly direction at first, later tending east towards the mountain ridges. A good 40min in from the road (at **1275m**), ignore the branch left ('Bavella par Chapelle', the return route) and keep right on what is now a path. A steepish but short

Looking back towards the Aiguilles de Bavella

climb amidst contorted pines brings you out on a particularly panoramic rise (1hr, 1315m), where the **Trou de la Bombe** or 'bomb hole' in the rock suddenly appears at close hand, sandwiched between the Calanca Murata and Punta Velaco to its south. The beautiful Aiguilles de Bavella can also be seen to the northwest.

Those with a sure foot and no vertigo problems can make their way around the rock face for the clamber up to the actual hole, which reveals a sheer 500m drop on the other side! Take great care.

Return to the **1275m junction** and turn right as per the 'Bavella par Chapelle' signs. Not far away is a rise known as Dame Jeanne, a good lookout for the Trou. Cows grazing among the ferns are commonly encountered on this stretch. The path drops to cross a stream. At the ensuing forks, follow the arrows through the pretty wood for the 'Chapelle', a reference to a small shrine in the vicinity. You end up on the surfaced road and will need to go left for the start point at **Col de Bavella** (1hr in descent).

13: Foce Finosa

Walking time	2hr 20min
Distance	5.3km/3.3 miles
Difficulty	Grade 2
Ascent/descent	400m/400m
Map	IGN scale 1:25,000 sheet 4253ET
Start/Finish	Auberge de Col de Bavella, Col de Bavella

This half-day walk follows a stretch of the long-distance trail GR20 as far as a mountain saddle which affords particularly fine views over rugged landscape. A tract of fairly steep terrain is entailed, and it can be especially slippery in wet conditions.

Close to the start point at the sheltered side of the

Punta Tafunata di i Paliri

road pass Col de Bavella is a scattering of curious low tin-roofed cabins like something out of film set. They are evidently the summertime dwellings of the residents of the village of Conca in the east, who were granted the land at the start of the 19th century by Napoleon III to enable them to find respite from the scorching heat of the malaria-ridden lowlands. Another version says they are shepherd's huts, one for every child from Conca for the duration of 99 years! ▶

See Walk 12 for route map, more information on the pass and on facilities at Col de Bavella.

Access: see Walk 12.

Close to the **Auberge de Col de Bavella** and the bend on the eastern flank of the Col de Bavella road pass (1218m), take the shady forestry track heading southeast marked with the red/white paint stripes of the GR20. After a water trough 10min along you are diverted off left for a steep and tiring but scenic descent through shrub vegetation. The striking Punta Tafunata di i Paliri can be seen east-northeast rearing up from a marvellous red-hued ridge, though its trademark hole, 'tafunata', is not visible from this angle.

137

Extension: Below northeast the shape of the Refuge Paliri hut can just be seen. At 1055m and some 45min downhill, it makes a worthwhile continuation as long as you remember it's uphill on the way back! Allow an extra 2hr.

On reaching the valley floor (1045m, 30min), a wide **forestry track** is joined around right (south) via a concrete concourse on a bend. Not far on a marked path breaks off east for the winding climb through beautiful forest carpeted with wild orchids to **Foce Finosa** (40min, 1206m). The saddle opens up in the mountainous ridge and you find yourself amongst dramatic rock formations, looking out east over a remarkably rugged valley. Don't neglect the panorama behind you to the Aiguilles, and north to outstanding M. Incudine, long reputed to be the favourite meeting place of female sorcerers who engaged in dreadful hunts for the souls of men! ◀

From Foce Finosa the walk returns the same way to the **Auberge de Col de Bavella** (1hr 10min, 1218m).

14: Zonza–Quenza Circuit

Walking time	4hr 20min
Distance	13.7km/8.6 miles
Difficulty	Grade 2
Ascent/descent	510m/510m
Map	IGN scale 1:25,000 sheets 4253OT, 4254OT
Start/Finish	Zonza

An **extension** is feasible to the intriguing prehistoric sites of Cucuruzzu and Capula – an extra 2hr 30min (see Walk 15) should be allowed.

A lovely varied loop-walk linking a string of quiet granite villages in the mountainous Alta Rocca region in the south of the island. At the foot of the spectacular Bavella rock needles this triangle-shaped route takes in deciduous woods with a great range of Mediterranean species, attractive watercourses, particularly suitable for a dip and a picnic on their shady banks, and lookouts over the rolling hills that characterise the area. ◀

The walk is straightforward on problem-free terrain, though the incessant ups and downs make it tiring. What's more, it's important to keep an eye out for the frequent if

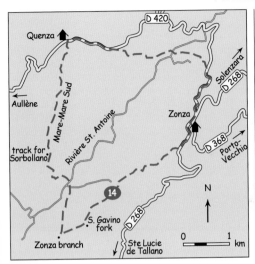

Facilities: The panoramically placed photogenic scattering of houses, shops, eateries and guesthouses that go under the name of Zonza makes a good base for exploring the region, including the magnificent Col de Bavella (see Walks 12 and 13). Hotels include L'Aiglon ☎ 04 9578 6779, open April–December, and Auberge du Sanglier ☎ 04 95786718, and there are also two camping grounds. Otherwise lovely Quenza has a hotel (Sole e Monti ☎ 04 95786253, open April–October), camping ground and *gîte d'étape* 1km east of the village, Odyssée ☎ 04 95786405, sleeps 36, open end March–October.

minimal changes of direction amidst the maze of hunter's tracks, though waymarking is adequate.

Those on the long-distance Mare-Mare Sud route can use this walk to detour via Zonza (whence Col de Bavella) and Quenza; slot in at the branch for Zonza in the concluding section of the description. ▶

Access: The modest hamlet of Zonza can be reached via the D368 from Porto-Vecchio, the narrow D268 Solenzara-Ste Lucie de Tallano or the D420 via Aullène. The Porto-Vecchio to Ajaccio minibus stops at Zonza.

From the four-way intersection at **Zonza** (744m), follow the D420 road north (Quenza direction) for 1km to a marked lane left at Fontanelle. A wood of old chestnut and oak precedes a scenic clearing before a drop to a bed of pebbles and a high bridge over the inviting waters of the **Rivière St Antoine** (625m). Tree heather, alder bushes and unusual ferns abound.

The twists and turns of an old path in gradual ascent are interrupted by the odd bulldozed stretch. On reaching

The Aiguilles de Bavella seen from the Quenza–Zonza path

the gate for a property, go right onto a farm track before picking up a lovely old path hemmed in by mossy stone walls and Mediterranean oaks where wild boar tracks abound. You emerge on the D420 in open farmland with lovely views of the Bavella rock needles. Follow the road left (west) past the turn-off for the *gîte d'étape,* then the Auberge Sole e Monti, and head into **Quenza** (1hr 15min, 820m), where you can collapse at one of the laid-back shady cafés.

The route continues west past the church then you swing left (south) to follow the Mare-Mare Sud signposts and orange waymarkers down past drinking troughs. Soon a narrow path off right alongside a stream with honeysuckle and wild mint drops to join a wider track through woods. There's an easy if lengthy stroll through lightly wooded farmland past a signed **track for Sorbollano**, concluding with a broom-lined lane leading to an enclosure for deer-breeding purposes. Here a path plunges left via a wire fence to a bridge over the **Rivière St Antoine** (1hr 15min, 568m). Close by a modest stream is forded, amidst bright orange lilies. After an ensuing climb through shady wood past old stone walls, you leave the Mare-Mare Sud route at the **Zonza branch** (30min, 730m).

Turn up left (northeast) for the steepish climb on a clay-based path to a panoramic rise scattered with granite boulders. A lane leads to a **fork for S. Gavino** – turn left here guided by stone sentinels to a pretty stretch along the banks of a stream. Going via a lane, you will eventually come out on the D268 road – turn left (north) towards the simple stone houses of nearby **Zonza** (1hr 20min, 744m).

15: Cucuruzzu and Capula Archaeological Sites

Walking time	1hr – but allow 2hr for the visit
Distance	2.3km/1.4 miles
Difficulty	Grade 1
Map	IGN scale 1:25,000 sheet 4254OT
Start/Finish	ticket booth, 5km west of Levie

One of Corsica's foremost archaeological sites, second only to Filitosa in the island's southwest, Cucuruzzu boasts a Bronze Age artisan settlement that dates back to the 1st–2nd millennium BC. Neighbouring Capula, on the other hand, was inhabited through the Iron Age and into medieval times. Between the two you see fortified structures in masonry, store rooms, lookout points, a burial site and a butcher's, not to mention an intriguing menhir. The natural setting itself makes a visit worthwhile – peaceful, romantic woodland punctuated by weird weathered granite rock shapes is brilliant with cyclamens and honeysuckle, added to which there are long-ranging views over the Alta Rocca villages, nestling in the wood-clad hills, and the marvellous backdrop of the Bavella rock needles. The walk is an easy affair on level ground for the most part, with ascent/descent of no consequence, and the paths are broad and clear. Training shoes would suffice.

These adjoining sites are manned from April through to October, around 9am through to sunset (though they

Facilities: The closest accommodation is at Levie – see the Mare-Mare Sud route, Day 2.

are not fenced off). The admission charge includes a walkman (*baladeur*) with a useful commentary in several languages, English included. A visit is also recommended to the Levie Archaeological Museum, which houses the 20,000 artefacts discovered on site. ◀

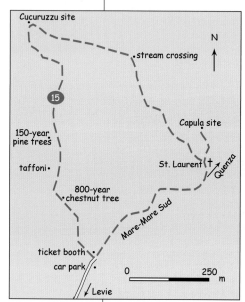

Access: By car leave the village of Levie west on the D268 (Ste. Lucie direction), and 3km along is a signposted turnoff for the 'Sites Archeologiques' on the Pianu de Levie. A further 2km will see you at the car park and the nearby ticket booth. On foot to this point it's 40min via the Mare-Mare Sud path. Levie itself can be reached by year-round bus from Ajaccio via Propriano.

Beginning from the **ticket booth**, or Accueil (760m), head north traversing a rather eerie wooded flat with gnarled trees and mossy banks reminiscent of *Lord of the Rings* scenery. Marker poles indicate points of special interest, such as a chestnut tree (point 2) that is a staggering 800 years old. Not far on (point 3) are the first curious *taffoni*, granite rock forms pierced by artistic holes that are the result of wind action. A couple of pine trees (point 5) are 150 years old, but their chief claim to fame is as a roost for the masses of pigeons which winter over in Corsica. Some 20min from the entrance comes the surprise of a clearing and **Cucuruzzu**. There's a so-called *casteddu*, akin to a prehistoric fortification or castle whose rock

Exploring the Cucuruzzu site

walls attain 5m in height, giving marvellous sweeping views over the surrounding rolling plain. Erstwhile weaving and pottery workshops, covered storage chambers, a round watch tower, and what may have been the chief's dwelling are among the highlights of an exploratory visit to this particularly evocative spot.

Back outside the walled enclosure, follow the arrows for points 12 and 13 east to ford a stream where wild garlic runs riot. A brief climb through a grassy clearing leads to a junction – keep left for the second site. A curious menhir with a sword-shaped engraving reminiscent of a cross stands guard at the foot of ramparts of **Capula**, shaded by massive oaks. Before the ascent itself, go left for an impressive Bronze Age rock shelter excavated in 1972. Then retrace your steps for the stone ramp which takes you to an extensive platform featuring a roofed area sheltering the alleged medieval abode of Count Bianco built on an Iron Age base, while the highest point overlooks the ruins of the main castle that was destroyed in 1259.

Go back down the ramp and continue straight ahead for the Romanesque chapel of St Laurent. Turn right onto the track for the 20min stroll back to the **ticket booth**.

16: Punta di a Vacca Morta

Walking time	1hr 40min
Distance	3.8km/2.4 miles
Difficulty	Grade 2–3
Ascent/descent	200m/200m
Map	IGN scale 1:25,000 sheet 4254ET
Start/Finish	Col de Mela

The modest 1314m summit of imaginatively named Punta di a Vacca Morta ('dead cow point') is a desolate windswept spot with marvellous views in all directions and a wealth of dwarf flowering plant life. It is renowned as one of Corsica's best lookouts. The walk involves a decent measure of height gain and loss and some elementary clambering, while extra attention is needed to track down the faded waymarks, few and far between.

It is described here as a fairly demanding but rewarding loop walk. A simpler alternative is to strike out up the crest as per the return route, and return the same way. Walkers on the long-distance Mare-Mare Sud can slot in at Foce Alta and exit at Col de Mela and resume their marked route. ◀

Facilities:
Accommodation in the area means the Catalavonu *gîte d'étape* Le Refuge ☎ 04 95700039, sleeps 44, open year-round. Excellent country-style meals.

Access: From the D368 (which links Porto-Vecchio with Zonza) on the southernmost corner of the Barrage de l'Ospedale lake, take the narrow road west. After 1.5km, where it veers south for Le Refuge at Cartalavonu, turn off right (north) for Col de Mela, keeping left (northwest) after 1km. The rough road ends at a hut, where you can park.

The Porto-Vecchio to Zonza summer bus service can be used as far as the lake.

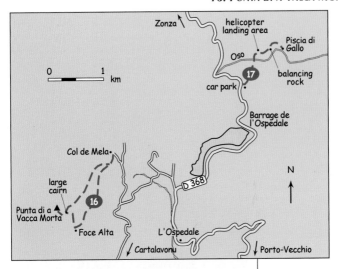

Once you've reached **Col de Mela** or Bocca a Mela (1068m) follow the forestry track southwest (Cartalavonu direction) marked with orange stripes for the Mare-Mare Sud. It is essentially on a level to the signposted saddle Foce Alta (1171m, 30min). Here you leave the main path for the faint route that breaks off north-northwest climbing steadily through the wood. Keep your eyes peeled for cairns, though unless it has become overgrown, the way is pretty recognisable. Some 10min from the turnoff (at around 1240m) you change direction and veer left (west). This is where the fun starts, as several rock formations need negotiating and you'll probably have to bash your way through the undergrowth of woody tree heather and broom. There's no path as such on this short stretch, but stone cairns point you continually upwards. You eventually and inevitably join one of the myriad paths heading left (west) along the ridge, past a **large cairn** atop a rock, to **Punta di a Vacca Morta** (1314m, 20min).

The amazingly vast views take in the Bavella massif and its needles, then M. Incudine to the north, and a multitude of villages in the Alta Rocca region, not to

Summit of Punta di a Vacca Morta

mention the coast and the Ospedale lake relatively close at hand below. What's more, the plant life merits inspection – a rare white type of thrift endemic to Corsica flourishes on the top amongst myriad prostrate shrubs, aromatic herbs and domes of broom. The setting, with weird wind-shaped rock formations and bent pines, invites thorough exploration.

For the descent route, return to the main ridge with the **large cairn** and proceed left (northeast). At the nearby fork keep straight ahead for the drop through rocks to open hillside studded with dwarf holly bushes, shaped by grazing livestock. Make your way towards the tumble of boulders then the barbed-wire fence which leads down to rejoin the track used at the start. Turn left onto the orange-marked route for the short distance back to **Col de Mela** (40min) once more.

17: Piscia di Gallo Waterfall

Walking time	1hr 15min
Distance	2.5km/1.6 miles
Difficulty	Grade 1–2
Ascent/descent	120m/120m
Map	IGN scale 1:25,000 sheet 4254ET
Start/Finish	car park 1km north of l'Ospedale dam

An absolutely stunning and justifiably popular walk to the waterfall known locally under the curious if denigrating name of the Piscia di Gallo or Ghjaddu ('the rooster's jet' or 'cascade'), an allusion to its contemptible or worthless nature in view of its limited flow. The drop is not that bad though – 70m down a sheer rock wall.

Within the reach of the average walker, this itinerary traverses beautiful forest studded with natural granite outcrops sculptured into wonderful forms by wind and rain, while the ridge section boasts marvellous wide-ranging views. Even if there has been an extended dry spell and waterfall flow is at a minimum, the walk is still worthwhile. If you intend extending the walk to the base of the fall, non-slip footwear is essential as there are steep stretches of terrain that can be wet and slippery.

An additional attraction in the vicinity is the Barrage de l'Ospedale, an artificial lake set in a steep-sided basin shaded by graceful pines. Constructed in 1979 to supply southern Corsica with water for drinking and irrigation, it is 135m long, 26m deep and has a 3 million m³ capacity. Neither boating nor swimming is allowed. ▶

Access: The D368 from Porto-Vecchio to Zonza will take you to the walk start, about 1km north of the wall of the Ospedale dam. The summer bus service on the same route will drop you here.

See Walk 16 for route map.

Facilities:
Refreshments are available at the many kiosks at the car park and walk start.
The closest accommodation is the gîte d'étape at Cartalavonu (Le Refuge (☎ 04 9570 0039, sleeps 44, open April to early October).

*Piscia di Gallo
waterfall*

From the **car park** (955m) and kiosks a clear marked path wastes no time dropping northeast to a forestry track and down to cross two streams with stepping stones. The ensuing climb leads to a helicopter landing area then continues northeast along a ridge above a stream. Waymarking is faded red paint and scarce, but stone cairns and pyramids point the way through this marvellous area of bizarrely shaped granite outcrops and elegant pines. An impressive **balancing rock** marks a great lookout over the sparkling coast. From here it's a brief clamber down to a good viewing point for the unusual **Piscia di Gallo** waterfall (836m, 30min). A jet of water formed by the Torrente Oso comes shooting out of a hole in the sheer rock face to crash onto a rock base below. You find yourself in a deep cool basin guarded by slender granite sentinels and lush vegetation.

A sign warns that this is the end of the marked path and anyone who continues does so at their own risk. So take great care if you decide to continue all the way down to the base of the fall, as it involves clambering over steep rock slabs and slippery terrain.

Return to the **car park** the same way (45min).

18: The White Cliffs of Bonifacio

Walking time	3hr
Distance	9km/5.6 miles
Difficulty	Grade 1
Map	IGN scale 1:25,000 sheet 4255OT
Start/Finish	waterfront car park in lower Bonifacio

An exciting walk to the southernmost point of Corsica along dramatic cliffs eroded crazily by the winds and seas that lash this coastline. One highlight is the extraordinary spectacle of the town of Bonifacio. It balances on the extremity of a crumbling limestone headland between a superb sheltered natural harbour and the Bouches de Bonifacio, the straits that separate French Corsica and Italian Sardinia. The walk destination is

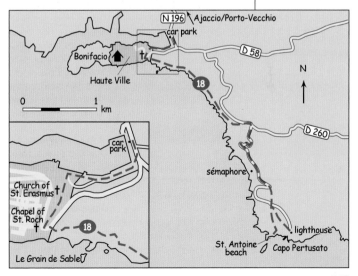

Bonifacio cliffs towards Capo Pertusato and its lighthouse

Capo Pertusato, its lighthouse and a beautiful beach. Considering that the area is exposed and windswept, there is a surprising array of vegetation, such as lilac sea rocket, showy oversized yellow daisies, rock samphire, aromatic everlasting, astragalus and rosemary.

On the remains of ancient Greek and Roman settlements, the town was 'officially' founded in the ninth century by Count Bonifacio from Tuscany on an expedition to free the island from Saracen invaders. In earlier mythological times it was supposedly visited by Ulysses: 'When we reached the harbour, we found it landlocked under steep cliffs, with a narrow entrance between two headlands' (Homer's *The Odyssey*). This turned out to be the rocky stronghold of the Laestrygonians, cannibalistic ogres! The reception is a tad warmer these days, though the prevailing winds can be chilling.

This walk is undeniably the most dramatic on offer in the area, but there are others within the town precincts as well as to neighbouring beaches – enquire at the Tourist Office ① 04 95731188.

Take plenty of sun cream, drinking water and, of course, swimming gear. No snack bars or eateries are encountered en route. Sports shoes (or light boots) are preferable as the terrain is rough and stony, though non-slip sandals are also feasible. The most strenuous part of the itinerary is probably the flight of stairs leading from the Bonifacio waterfront to the Chapel of St Roch, otherwise height gain and loss are negligible. ▶

Access: Bonifacio can be reached by car or year-round coach from Ajaccio or Porto-Vecchio, and by ferry from Santa Teresa Gallura in Sardinia (Italy).

The main car park, bus stop and walk start are to be found on the waterfront in the lower part of Bonifacio where the N196 terminates. Some buses continue for the climb to the historic Haute Ville (upper town), so travellers who stay on board can join the walk at the Chapel of St Roch.

Starting at the **car park** in lower Bonifacio, leave the road to follow the quaysides flanking the Port de Plaisance (marina) and head west towards the imposing Haute Ville. After several inviting waterside restaurants, take the broad flight of stairs, Montée Rastello, beneath the 13th-century church dedicated to the patron saint of sailors and fishermen, St Erasmus. This brings you out at the road below the massive Genoese citadel, not to mention a saddle and break in the 60m high cliff-line. Overlooking the sea and an odd eroded rock island known as Le Grain de Sable ('grain of sand') stands the **Chapel of St Roch** (15min), which commemorates the last victim of the terrible 1528 plague that slashed the population from 5000 to 700.

Unless you're ready for a swim at the Plage de Sotto-Rocca below, turn left up the sloping paved pathway that climbs easily away from the town to the top of the stunning cliffs or *falaises* which stretch out ahead. Low-set pillars with artistic ceramic plaques act as path markers and there are lookout points galore. The wind-blown terrain is anchored by low maquis cover with aromatic herbs and salt-resistant plants. From this angle the town looks even more precarious, overhanging crumbling

Facilities: Bonifacio has a broad range of accommodation including a camping ground and Hotel Le Royal ☎ 04 95730051. Tourist Office ① 04 95731188.

St Antoine beach

strata that are gradually being worn away, with massive blocks already having careened off into the sea.

The path follows the coastline on the initial part, with a brief detour inland to a house at a road junction with the D260 (40min from St Roch) where you turn right signed for Pertusato. At the ensuing bend a faint path drops to an attractive beach – but it's worth waiting for your swim.

Not far on are ruined fortifications dating back to the Second World War, then a military signal station (*sémaphore*). At the next bend in the road you head up through shrubs to cut the corner. On the ridge is the access path dropping to the simply stunning cove with the white sand of **St Antoine beach** – a compulsory descent.

Afterwards, a path continues south along the headland for the lighthouse on **Capo Pertusato** (1hr 30min total). From here it's a mere 12km (7.5 miles) stone's throw across the water to Sardinia. The famed Archipel des Lavezzi, a nature reserve, lies to the southeast.

Return at your leisure the same way to **Bonifacio**.

LONG-DISTANCE ROUTE SUMMARIES

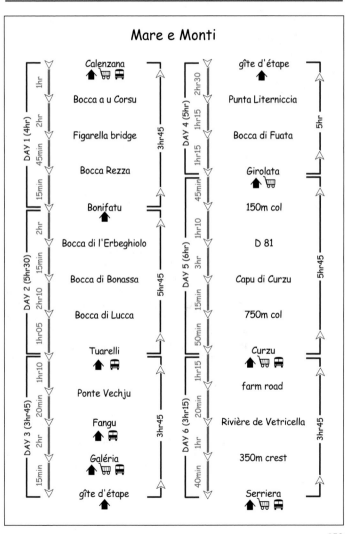

Mare e Monti

DAY 1 (4hr)
- Calenzana — 1hr
- Bocca a u Corsu — 2hr
- Figarella bridge — 45min
- Bocca Rezza — 15min
- Bonifatu

(3hr45)

DAY 2 (5hr30)
- Bonifatu — 2hr
- Bocca di l'Erbeghiolo — 15min
- Bocca di Bonassa — 2hr10
- Bocca di Lucca — 1hr05
- Tuarelli

(5hr45)

DAY 3 (3hr45)
- Tuarelli — 1hr10
- Ponte Vechju — 20min
- Fangu — 2hr
- Galéria — 15min
- gîte d'étape

(3hr45)

DAY 4 (5hr)
- gîte d'étape — 2hr30
- Punta Literniccia — 1hr15
- Bocca di Fuata — 1hr15
- Girolata

(5hr)

DAY 5 (6hr)
- Girolata — 45min
- 150m col — 1hr10
- D 81 — 3hr
- Capu di Curzu — 15min
- 750m col — 50min
- Curzu

(5hr45)

DAY 6 (3hr15)
- Curzu — 1hr15
- farm road — 20min
- Rivière de Vetricella — 1hr
- 350m crest — 40min
- Serriera

(3hr45)

Mare e Monti

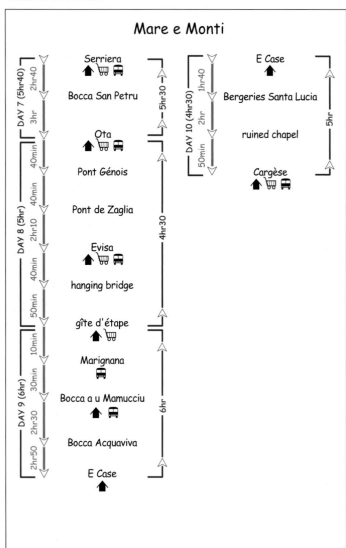

Mare-Mare Nord

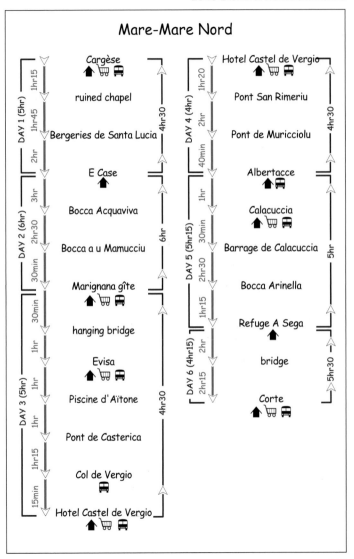

DAY 1 (5hr) — 1hr15 / 1hr45

Cargèse

ruined chapel

Bergeries de Santa Lucia

DAY 2 (6hr) — 2hr / 3hr / 2hr30 / 30min

E Case

Bocca Acquaviva

Bocca a u Mamucciu

Marignana gîte

DAY 3 (5hr) — 30min / 1hr / 1hr / 1hr15 / 15min

hanging bridge

Evisa

Piscine d'Aïtone

Pont de Casterica

Col de Vergio

Hotel Castel de Vergio

4hr30 / 6hr / 4hr30

DAY 4 (4hr) — 1hr20 / 2hr / 40min

Hotel Castel de Vergio

Pont San Rimeriu

Pont de Muricciolu

Albertacce

DAY 5 (5hr15) — 1hr / 30min / 2hr30

Calacuccia

Barrage de Calacuccia

Bocca Arinella

DAY 6 (4hr15) — 1hr15 / 2hr / 2hr15

Refuge A Sega

bridge

Corte

4hr30 / 5hr / 5hr30

Mare-Mare Nord

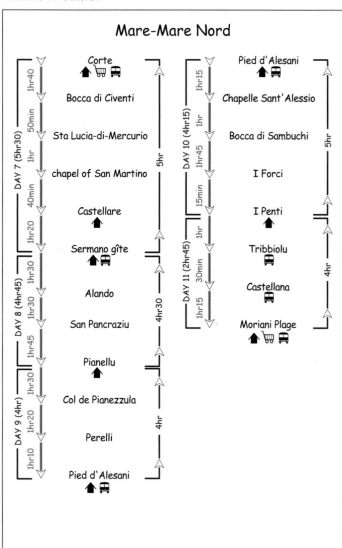

DAY 7 (5hr30)
- Corte — 1hr40
- Bocca di Civenti — 50min
- Sta Lucia-di-Mercurio — 1hr
- chapel of San Martino — 40min
- Castellare — 1hr20

DAY 8 (4hr45)
- Sermano gîte — 1hr30
- Alando — 1hr30
- San Pancraziu — 1hr45
- Pianellu — 1hr30

DAY 9 (4hr)
- Col de Pianezzula — 1hr20
- Perelli — 1hr10
- Pied d'Alesani

(Corte to Sermano gîte: 5hr / 4hr30)
(to Pied d'Alesani: 4hr)

DAY 10 (4hr15)
- Pied d'Alesani — 1hr15
- Chapelle Sant'Alessio — 1hr
- Bocca di Sambuchi — 1hr45
- I Forci — 15min
- I Penti

DAY 11 (2hr45)
- Tribbiolu — 1hr
- Castellana — 30min
- Moriani Plage — 1hr15

(Pied d'Alesani to I Penti: 5hr)
(I Penti to Moriani Plage: 4hr)

Mare-Mare Sud

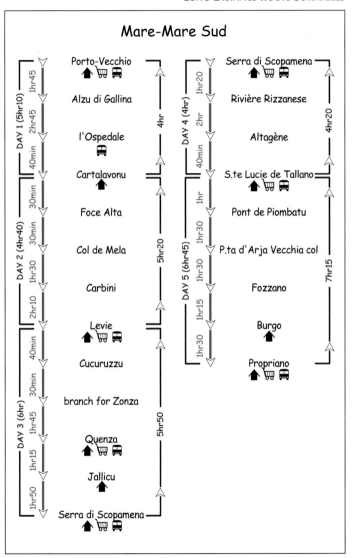

GLOSSARY OF FRENCH AND CORSICAN TERMS

accueil	reception, ticket booth	chemin de fer	railway
acqua	water	coin cuisine	cooking facilities
aiguille	rock needle	col	mountain pass
alimentation	grocery store	complet	full (for lodging)
aller/retour	outward/return trip	couchette	bunk bed
auberge	hotel, guesthouse	coup de soleil	sunstroke
au secours!	help!	courbe	bend
autocar, car	bus	couvent	convent
auto-stop	hitchhiking	crête	ridge
bain	bath	croix	cross, crucifix
balade	stroll, walk	dangereux	dangerous
balisé	waymarked	défilé	ravine, gorge
barrage	dam	demi-pension	half board
bateau	boat, ship	départ	start point
belvédère	scenic lookout point	dîner	evening meal
bergerie	shepherd's hut	distributeur automatique de billets	automatic teller machine, ATM
bière pression	draft beer		
bocca	pass (*literally* mouth)	dortoir	dormitory
bois	wood	douche	shower
boucle	loop	drap	sheet (for bed)
boulangerie	bakery	droit	right (direction)
boussole	compass	eau potable	drinking water
buvette	snack bar	école	school
capo, capu	cape, mountain	église	church
car	bus, coach	épicerie	grocery store
carte	map	étape	walk stage
casa	house	facile	easy
cascade	waterfall	falaise	cliff
casse-croûte	snack	fermé	closed
chambre	bedroom	fleuve	river
chambre d'hôte	bed and breakfast	foce	col
chasse	hunting	fontaine	spring, drinking water
châtaigne	chestnut	gare	railway station
chemin	path, way		

gauche	left (direction)	pont	bridge
gibier	game (animals)	portable	mobile phone
gîte d'étape	walker's hostel	punta	rock point
grotte	cave	raide	steep
hameau	hamlet	randonnée pédestre	walking
hébergement	accommodation	ravin	ravine
horaire	timetable	ravitaillement	provisions
Hôtel de Ville, Mairie	Town Hall	refuge	basic hut for hikers
lacets	zigzags	renseignements	information
lavoir	trough	restauration	meals
libre-service	self-service grocery store	rive	river bank
littoral	coast	rivière	river
en location	for rent	route	road
maison	house	ruisseau	stream
montée	ascent	sac à dos	rucksack
moulin	mill	sac à viande	sleeping sheet, bag liner
météo	weather forecast	sac de couchage	sleeping bag
muletier	mule track	sanglier	boar
navette	shuttle service	secours	rescue
neige	snow	sémaphore	signal station
névé	permanent snow	sentier	path
orage	storm	sommet	summit of mountain
ouvert	open	source	spring (water)
pain	bread	table d'orientation	orientation table
panier-repas	packed lunch	tarif	fare
passerelle suspendue	hanging bridge	torrent	mountain stream
pays	village	tour	tower
pente	slope	vallée	valley
petit-déjeuner	breakfast	vent	wind
phare	lighthouse	vente de fromage	cheese for sale
pharmacie	chemist	ville	town
piscine	swimming pool or rock pool	voie sans issue	dead-end road
piste	unsurfaced road, lane		
plage	beach		
pluie	rain		

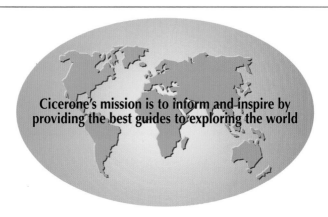

Cicerone's mission is to inform and inspire by providing the best guides to exploring the world

Since its foundation 40 years ago, Cicerone has specialised in publishing guidebooks and has built a reputation for quality and reliability. It now publishes nearly 300 guides to the major destinations for outdoor enthusiasts, including Europe, UK and the rest of the world.

Written by leading and committed specialists, Cicerone guides are recognised as the most authoritative. They are full of information, maps and illustrations so that the user can plan and complete a successful and safe trip or expedition – be it a long face climb, a walk over Lakeland fells, an alpine cycling tour, a Himalayan trek or a ramble in the countryside.

With a thorough introduction to assist planning, clear diagrams, maps and colour photographs to illustrate the terrain and route, and accurate and detailed text, Cicerone guides are designed for ease of use and access to the information.

If the facts on the ground change, or there is any aspect of a guide that you think we can improve, we are always delighted to hear from you.

Cicerone Press
2 Police Square Milnthorpe Cumbria LA7 7PY
Tel: 015395 62069 Fax: 015395 63417
info@cicerone.co.uk www.cicerone.co.uk